First Workshop on Trustworthy Natural Language Processing (TrustNLP 2021)

Online
10 June 2021

ISBN: 978-1-7138-3032-0

Printed from e-media with permission by:

Curran Associates, Inc.
57 Morehouse Lane
Red Hook, NY 12571

Some format issues inherent in the e-media version may also appear in this print version.

Printed with permission by Curran Associates, Inc. (2021)

For permission requests, please contact the Association for Computational Linguistics at the address below.

Association for Computational Linguistics
209 N. Eighth Street
Stroudsburg, Pennsylvania 18360

Phone: 1-570-476-8006
Fax: 1-570-476-0860

acl@aclweb.org

Additional copies of this publication are available from:

Curran Associates, Inc.
57 Morehouse Lane
Red Hook, NY 12571 USA
Phone: 845-758-0400
Fax: 845-758-2633
Email: curran@proceedings.com
Web: www.proceedings.com

TrustNLP: First Workshop on Trustworthy Natural Language Processing

Proceedings of the Workshop

June 10, 2021

Introduction

Recent progress in Artificial Intelligence (AI) and Natural Language Processing (NLP) has greatly increased their presence in everyday consumer products in the last decade. Common examples include virtual assistants, recommendation systems, and personal healthcare management systems, among others. Advancements in these fields have historically been driven by the goal of improving model performance as measured by accuracy, but recently the NLP research community has started incorporating additional constraints to make sure models are fair and privacy-preserving. However, these constraints are not often considered together, which is important since there are critical questions at the intersection of these constraints such as the tension between simultaneously meeting privacy objectives and fairness objectives, which requires knowledge about the demographics a user belongs to. In this workshop, we aim to bring together these distinct yet closely related topics.

We invited papers which focus on developing models that are "explainable, fair, privacy-preserving, causal, and robust" (Trustworthy ML Initiative). Topics of interest include:

- Differential Privacy
- Fairness and Bias: Evaluation and Treatments
- Model Explainability and Interpretability
- Accountability
- Ethics
- Industry applications of Trustworthy NLP
- Causal Inference
- Secure and trustworthy data generation

In total, we accepted 11 papers, including 2 non-archival papers. We hope all the attendants enjoy this workshop.

Organizing Committee

- Yada Pruksachatkun - Alexa AI
- Anil Ramakrishna - Alexa AI
- Kai-Wei Chang - UCLA, Amazon Visiting Academic
- Satyapriya Krishna - Alexa AI
- Jwala Dhamala - Alexa AI
- Tanaya Guha - University of Warwick
- Xiang Ren - USC

Speakers

- Mandy Korpusik - Assistant professor, Loyola Marymount University
- Richard Zemel - Industrial Research Chair in Machine Learning, University of Toronto
- Robert Monarch - Author, Human-in-the-Loop Machine Learning

Program committee

- Rahul Gupta - Alexa AI
- Willie Boag - Massachusetts Institute of Technology
- Naveen Kumar - Disney Research
- Nikita Nangia - New York University
- He He - New York University
- Jieyu Zhao - University of California Los Angeles
- Nanyun Peng - University of California Los Angeles
- Spandana Gella - Alexa AI
- Moin Nadeem - Massachusetts Institute of Technology
- Maarten Sap - University of Washington
- Tianlu Wang - University of Virginia
- William Wang - University of Santa Barbara
- Joe Near - University of Vermont
- David Darais - Galois
- Pratik Gajane - Department of Computer Science, Montanuniversitat Leoben, Austria
- Paul Pu Liang - Carnegie Mellon University

- Hila Gonen - Bar-Ilan University
- Patricia Thaine - University of Toronto
- Jamie Hayes - Google DeepMind, University College London, UK
- Emily Sheng - University of California Los Angeles
- Isar Nejadgholi - National Research Council Canada
- Anthony Rios - University of Texas at San Antonio

Table of Contents

Conference Program

June 10, 2021

9:00–9:10 *Opening*
Organizers

9:10–10:00 *Keynote 1*
Richard Zemel

10:00–11:00 Paper Presentations

Interpretability Rules: Jointly Bootstrapping a Neural Relation Extractorwith an Explanation Decoder
Zheng Tang and Mihai Surdeanu

Measuring Biases of Word Embeddings: What Similarity Measures and Descriptive Statistics to Use?
Hossein Azarpanah and Mohsen Farhadloo

Private Release of Text Embedding Vectors
Oluwaseyi Feyisetan and Shiva Kasiviswanathan

Accountable Error Characterization
Amita Misra, Zhe Liu and Jalal Mahmud

11:00–11:15 ***Break***

June 10, 2021 (continued)

11:15–12:15 Paper Presentations

xER: An Explainable Model for Entity Resolution using an Efficient Solution for the Clique Partitioning Problem
Samhita Vadrevu, Rakesh Nagi, JinJun Xiong and Wen-mei Hwu

Gender Bias in Natural Language Processing Across Human Languages
Abigail Matthews, Isabella Grasso, Christopher Mahoney, Yan Chen, Esma Wali, Thomas Middleton, Mariama Njie and Jeanna Matthews

Interpreting Text Classifiers by Learning Context-sensitive Influence of Words
Sawan Kumar, Kalpit Dixit and Kashif Shah

Towards Benchmarking the Utility of Explanations for Model Debugging
Maximilian Idahl, Lijun Lyu, Ujwal Gadiraju and Avishek Anand

12:15–1:30 ***Lunch Break***

13:00–14:00 ***Mentorship Meeting***

14:00–14:50 *Keynote 2*
Mandy Korpusik

14:50–15:00 ***Break***

15:00–16:00 ***Poster Session***

16:15–17:05 *Keynote 3*
Robert Munro

17:05–17:15 ***Closing Address***

Interpretability Rules: Jointly Bootstrapping a Neural Relation Extractor with an Explanation Decoder

Zheng Tang, Mihai Surdeanu
Department of Computer Science
University of Arizona, Tucson, Arizona, USA
{zhengtang, msurdeanu}@email.arizona.edu

Abstract

We introduce a method that transforms a rule-based relation extraction (RE) classifier into a neural one such that both interpretability and performance are achieved. Our approach jointly trains a RE classifier with a decoder that generates explanations for these extractions, using as sole supervision a set of rules that match these relations. Our evaluation on the TACRED dataset shows that our neural RE classifier outperforms the rule-based one we started from by 9 F1 points; our decoder generates explanations with a high BLEU score of over 90%; and, the joint learning improves the performance of both the classifier and decoder.

1 Introduction

Information extraction (IE) is one of the key challenges in the natural language processing (NLP) field. With the explosion of unstructured information on the Internet, the demand for high-quality tools that convert free text to structured information continues to grow (Chang et al., 2010; Lee et al., 2013; Valenzuela-Escarcega et al., 2018).

The past decades have seen a steady transition from rule-based IE systems (Appelt et al., 1993) to methods that rely on machine learning (ML) (see Related Work). While this transition has generally yielded considerable performance improvements, it was not without a cost. For example, in contrast to modern deep learning methods, the predictions of rule-based approaches are easily explainable, as a small number of rules tends to apply to each extraction. Further, in many situations, rule-based methods can be developed by domain experts with minimal training data. For these reasons, rule-based IE methods remain widely used in industry (Chiticariu et al., 2013).

In this work we demonstrate that this transition from rule- to ML-based IE can be performed such that the benefits of both worlds are preserved. In particular, we start with a rule-based relation extraction (RE) system (Angeli et al., 2015) and bootstrap a neural RE approach that is trained jointly with a decoder that learns to generate the rules that best explain each particular extraction. The contributions of our idea are the following:

(1) We introduce a strategy that jointly learns a RE classifier between pairs of entity mentions with a decoder that generates explanations for these extractions in the form of Tokensregex (Chang and Manning, 2014) or Semregex (Chambers et al., 2007) patterns. The only supervision for our method is a set of input rules (or patterns) in these two frameworks (Angeli et al., 2015), which we use to generate positive examples for both the classifier and the decoder. We generate negative examples automatically from the sentences that contain positives examples.

(2) We evaluate our approach on the TACRED dataset (Zhang et al., 2017) and demonstrate that: (a) our neural RE classifier outperforms considerably the rule-based one we started from; (b) our decoder generates explanations with high accuracy, i.e., a BLEU overlap score between the generated rules and the gold, hand-written rules of over 90%; and, (c) joint learning improves the performance of both the classifier and decoder.

(3) We demonstrate that our approach generalizes to the situation where a vast amount of labeled training data is combined with a few rules. We combined the TACRED training data with the above rules and showed that when our method is trained on this combined data, the classifier obtains near state-of-art performance at 67.0% F1, while the decoder generates accurate explanations with a BLEU score of 92.4%.

2 Related Work

Relation extraction using statistical methods is well studied. Methods range from supervised, "traditional" approaches (Zelenko et al., 2003;

Proceedings of the First Workshop on Trustworthy Natural Language Processing, pages 1–7
June 10, 2021. ©2021 Association for Computational Linguistics

Bunescu and Mooney, 2005) to neural methods. Neural approaches for RE range from methods that rely on simpler representations such as CNNs (Zeng et al., 2014) and RNNs (Zhang and Wang, 2015) to more complicated ones such as augmenting RNNs with different components (Xu et al., 2015; Zhou et al., 2016), combining RNNs and CNNs (Vu et al., 2016; Wang et al., 2016), and using mechanisms like attention (Zhang et al., 2017) or GCNs (Zhang et al., 2018). To solve the lack of annotated data, distant supervision (Mintz et al., 2009; Surdeanu et al., 2012) is commonly used to generate a training dataset from an existing knowledge base. Jat et al. (2018) address the inherent noise in distant supervision with an entity attention method.

Rule-based methods in IE have also been extensively investigated. Riloff (1996) developed a system that learns extraction patterns using only a pre-classified corpus of relevant and irrelevant texts. Lin and Pantel (2001) proposed a unsupervised method for discovering inference rules from text based on the Harris distributional similarity hypothesis (Harris, 1954). Valenzuela-Escárcega et al. (2016) introduced a rule language that covers both surface text and syntactic dependency graphs. Angeli et al. (2015) further show that converting rule-based models to statistical ones can capture some of the benefits of both, i.e., the precision of patterns and the generalizability of statistical models.

Interpretability has gained more attention recently in the ML/NLP community. For example, some efforts convert neural models to more interpretable ones such as decision trees (Craven and Shavlik, 1996; Frosst and Hinton, 2017). Some others focus on producing a post-hoc explanation of individual model outputs (Ribeiro et al., 2016; Hendricks et al., 2016).

Inspired by these directions, here we propose an approach that combines the interpretability of rule-based methods with the performance and generalizability of neural approaches.

3 Approach

Our approach jointly addresses classification and interpretability through an encoder-decoder architecture, where the decoder uses multi-task learning (MTL) for relation extraction between pairs of named entities (Task 1) and rule generation (Task 2). Figure 1 summarizes our approach.

3.1 Task 1: Relation Classifier

We define the RE task as follows. The inputs consist of a sentence $W = [w_1, \ldots, w_n]$, and a pair of entities (called "subject" and "object") corresponding to two spans in this sentence: $W_s = [w_{s_1}, \ldots, w_{s_n}]$ and $W_o = [w_{o_1}, \ldots, w_{o_n}]$. The goal is to predict a relation $r \in R$ (from a predefined set of relation types) that holds between the subject and object or "no relation" otherwise.

For each sentence, we associate each word w_i with a representation $\boldsymbol{x}_i$ that concatenates three embeddings: $\boldsymbol{x}_i = \boldsymbol{e}(w_i) \circ \boldsymbol{e}(n_i) \circ \boldsymbol{e}(p_i)$, where $\boldsymbol{e}(w_i)$ is the word embedding of token i, $\boldsymbol{e}(n_i)$ is the NER embedding of token i, $\boldsymbol{e}(p_i)$ is the POS Tag embedding of token i. We feed these representations into a sentence-level bidirectional LSTM encoder (Hochreiter and Schmidhuber, 1997):

$$[\boldsymbol{h}_1, \ldots, \boldsymbol{h}_n] = \text{LSTM}([\boldsymbol{x}_1, \ldots, \boldsymbol{x}_n]) \tag{1}$$

Following (Zhang et al., 2018), we extract the "K-1 pruned" dependency tree that covers the two entities, i.e., the shortest dependency path between two entities enhanced with all tokens that are directly attached to the path, and feed it into a GCN (Kipf and Welling, 2016) layer:

$$\boldsymbol{h}_i^{(l)} = \sigma(\sum_{j=1}^{n} \tilde{A}_{ij} \boldsymbol{W}^{(l)} \boldsymbol{h}_j^{(l-1)} / d_i + \boldsymbol{b}^{(l)}) \tag{2}$$

where $\boldsymbol{A}$ is the corresponding adjacency matrix, $\tilde{\boldsymbol{A}} = \boldsymbol{A} + \boldsymbol{I}$ with $\boldsymbol{I}$ being the $n \times n$ identity matrix, $d_i = \sum_{j=1}^{n} \tilde{A}_{ij}$ is the degree of token i in the resulting graph, and $\boldsymbol{W}^{(l)}$ is linear transformation.

Lastly, we concatenate the sentence representation, the subject entity representation, and the object entity representation as follows:

$$\boldsymbol{h}_{sent} = f(\boldsymbol{h}^{(L)}) = f(\text{GCN}(\boldsymbol{h}^{(0)})) \tag{3}$$

$$\boldsymbol{h}_s = f(\boldsymbol{h}_{s_1:s_n}^{(L)}) \tag{4}$$

$$\boldsymbol{h}_o = f(\boldsymbol{h}_{o_1:o_n}^{(L)}) \tag{5}$$

$$\boldsymbol{h}_{final} = \boldsymbol{h}_{sent} \circ \boldsymbol{h}_s \circ \boldsymbol{h}_o \tag{6}$$

where $\boldsymbol{h}^{(l)}$ denotes the collective hidden representations at layer l of the GCN, and $f : \mathbb{R}^{d \times n} \to \mathbb{R}^d$ is a max pooling function that maps from n output vectors to the representation vector. The concatenated representation $\boldsymbol{h}_{final}$ is fed to a feed-forward layer with a softmax function to produce a probability distribution over relation types.

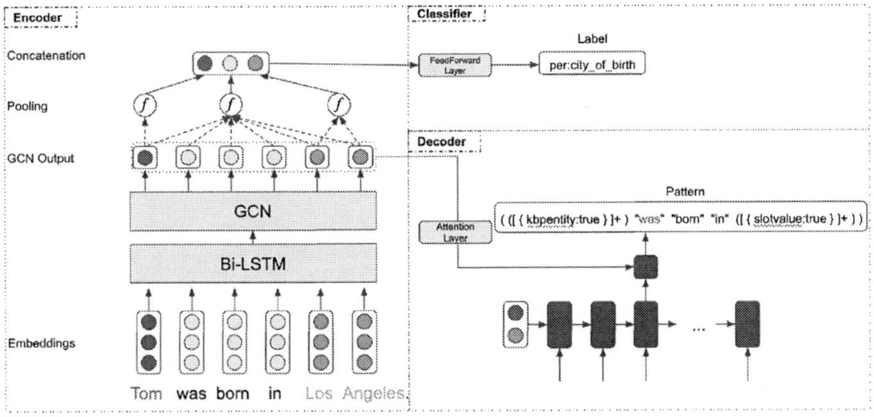

Figure 1: Neural architecture of the proposed multitask learning approach. The input is a sequence of words together with NER labels and POS tags. The pair of entities to be classified ("subject" in blue and "object" in orange) are also provided. We use a concatenation of several representations, including embeddings of words, NER labels, and POS tags. The encoder uses a sentence-level bidirectional LSTM (biLSTM) and graph convolutional networks (GCN). There are pooling layers for the subject, object, and full sentence GCN outputs. The concatenated pooling outputs are fed to the classifier's feedforward layer. The decoder is an LSTM with an attention mechanism.

3.2 Task 2: Rule Decoder

The rule decoder's goal is to generate the pattern P that extracted the corresponding data point, where P is represented as a sequence of tokens in the corresponding pattern language: $P = [p_1, \ldots, p_n]$. For example, the pattern `(([{kbpentity:true}]+)/was/ /born/ /on/([{slotvalue:true}]+))` (where `kbpentity:true` marks subject tokens, and `slotvalue:true` marks object tokens) extracts mentions of the `per:date_of_birth` relation.

We implemented this decoder using an LSTM with an attention mechanism. To center rule decoding around the subject and object, we first feed the concatenation of subject and object representation from the encoder as the initial state in the decoder. Then, in each timestep t, we generate the attention context vector $\boldsymbol{C}_t^D$ by using the current hidden state of the decoder, $\boldsymbol{h}_t^D$:

$$\boldsymbol{s}_t(j) = \boldsymbol{h}_{(L)}^E \boldsymbol{W}^A \boldsymbol{h}_t^D \tag{7}$$

$$\boldsymbol{a}_t = \text{softmax}(\boldsymbol{s}_t) \tag{8}$$

$$\boldsymbol{C}_t^D = \sum_j \boldsymbol{a}_t(j) \boldsymbol{h}_j^E \tag{9}$$

where $\boldsymbol{W}^A$ is a learned matrix, and $\boldsymbol{h}_{(L)}^E$ are hidden representations from the encoder's GCN.

We feed this $\boldsymbol{C}_t^D$ vector to a single feed forward layer that is coupled with a softmax function and use its output to obtain a probability distribution over the pattern vocabulary.

We use cross entropy to calculate the losses for both the classifier and decoder. To balance the loss between classifier and decoder, we normalize the decoder loss by the pattern length. Note that for the data points without an existing rule, we only calculate the classifier loss. Formally, the joint loss function is:

$$\text{loss} = \text{loss}_c + \text{loss}_d / length(P) \tag{10}$$

Approach	Precision	Recall	F1	BLEU
	Rule-only data			
Rule baseline	**86.9**	23.2	36.6	–
Our approach	60.0	**36.7**	**45.5**	**90.3**
w/o decoder	58.7	36.4	44.9	–
w/o classifier	–	–	–	88.3
	Rules + TACRED training data			
C-GCN	69.9	63.3	66.4	–
Our approach	70.2	**64.0**	**67.0**	**92.4**
w/o decoder	**71.2**	62.3	66.5	–
w/o classifier	–	–	–	91.6

Table 1: Results on the TACRED test partition, including ablation experiments (the "w/o" rows). We experimented with two configurations: *Rule-only data* uses only training examples generated by rules; *Rules + TACRED training data* applies the previous rules to the training dataset from TACRED.

4 Experiments

Data Preparation: We report results on the TACRED dataset (Zhang et al., 2017). We bootstrap

Hand-written Rule	Decoded Rule
(([{kbpentity:true}]+)""" based ""in"([{slotvalue:true}]+))	(([{kbpentity:true}]+)"in"([{slotvalue:true}]+))
(([{kbpentity:true}]+)" CEO "([{slotvalue:true}]+))	(([{kbpentity:true}]+)" president "([{slotvalue:true}]+))

Table 2: Examples of mistakes in the decoded rules. We highlight in the hand-written rules the tokens that were missed during decoding (false negatives) in green, and in the decoded rules we highlight the spurious tokens (false positives) in red.

Model	Precision	Recall	F1	BLEU
20% of rules	74.9	20.1	31.7	96.9
40% of rules	69.0	26.9	38.8	90.8
60% of rules	62.7	29.7	40.3	88.8
80% of rules	57.3	36.5	44.6	89.4

Table 3: Learning curve of our approach based on amount of rules used, in the *rule-only data* configuration. These results are on TACRED development.

our models from the patterns in the rule-based system of Angeli et al. (2015), which uses 4,528 surface patterns (in the Tokensregex language) and 169 patterns over syntactic dependencies (using Semgrex). We experimented with two configurations: *rule-only data* and *rules + TACRED training data*. In the former setting, we use solely positive training examples generated by the above rules. We combine these positive examples with negative ones generated automatically by assigning 'no_relation' to all other entity mention pairs in the same sentence where there is a positive example.[1] We generated 3,850 positive and 12,311 negative examples for this configuration. In the latter configuration, we apply the same rules to the entire TACRED training dataset.[2]

Baselines: We compare our approach with two baselines: the rule-based system of Zhang et al. (2017), and the best non-combination method of Zhang et al. (2018). The latter method uses an LSTM and GCN combination similar to our encoder.[3]

Implementation Details: We use pre-trained GloVe vectors (Pennington et al., 2014) to initialize our word embeddings. We use the *Adagrad* optimizer (Duchi et al., 2011). We apply entity masking to subject and object entities in the sentence, which is replacing the original token with a special `<NER>`–SUBJ or `<NER>`–OBJ token where `<NER>` is the corresponding name entity label provided by TACRED.

We used micro precision, recall, and F1 scores to evaluate the RE classifier. We used the BLEU score to measure the quality of generated rules, i.e., how close they are to the corresponding gold rules that extracted the same output. We used the BLEU implementation in NLTK (Loper and Bird, 2002), which allows us to calculate multi-reference BLEU scores over 1 to 4 grams.[4] We report BLEU scores only over the non 'no_relation' extractions with the corresponding testing data points that are matched by one of the rules in (Zhang et al., 2017).

Results and Discussion: Table 1 reports the overall performance of our approach, the baselines, and ablation settings, for the two configurations investigated. We draw the following observations from these results:

(1) The rule-based method of Zhang et al. (2017) has high precision but suffers from low recall. In contrast, our approach that is bootstrapped from the same information has 13% higher recall and almost 9% higher F1 (absolute). Further, our approach decodes explanatory rules with a high BLEU score of 90%, which indicates that it maintains almost the entire explanatory power of the rule-based method.

(2) The ablation experiments indicate that *joint* training for classification and explainability helps both tasks, in both configurations. This indicates that performance and explainability are interconnected.

(3) The two configurations analyzed in the table demonstrate that our approach performs well not only when trained solely on rules, but also when rules are combined with a training dataset annotated for RE. This suggests that our direction may

[1]During the generation of these negative examples we filtered out pairs corresponding to inverse and symmetric relations. For example, if a sentence contains a relation (Subj, Rel, Obj), we do not generate the negative (Obj, no_relation, Subj) if Rel has an inverse relation, e.g., `per:children` is the inverse of `per:parents`.

[2]Thus, some training examples in this case will be associated with a rule and some will not. We adjusted the loss function to use only the classification loss when no rule applies.

[3]For a fair comparison, we do not compare against ensemble methods, or transformer-based ones. Also, note that this baseline does *not* use rules at all.

[4]We scored longer n-grams to better capture rule syntax.

be a general strategy to infuse some explainability in a statistical method, when rules are available during training.

(4) Table 3 lists the learning curve for our approach in the *rule-only data* configuration when the amount of rules available varies.[5] This table shows that our approach obtains a higher F1 than the complete rule-based RE classifier even when using only 40% of the rules.[6]

(5) Note that the BLEU score provides an incomplete evaluation of rule quality. To understand if the decoded rules explain their corresponding data point, we performed a manual evaluation on 176 decoded rules. We classified them into three categories: (a) the rules correctly explain the prediction (according to the human annotator), (b) they approximately explain the prediction, and (c) they do not explain the prediction. Class (b) contains rules that do not lexically match the input text, but capture the correct semantics, as shown in Table 2. The percentages we measured were: (a) 33.5%, (b) 31.3%, (c) 26.1%. 9% of these rules were skipped in the evaluation because they were false negatives(which are labeled as no relation falsely by our model). These numbers support our hypothesis that, in general, the decoded rules do explain the classifier's prediction.

Further, out of 750 data points associated with rules in the evaluation data, our method incorrectly classifies only 26. Out of these 26, 16 were false negatives, and had no rules decoded. In the other 10 predictions, 7 rules fell in class (b) (see the examples in Table 2). The other 3 were incorrect due to ambiguity, i.e., the pattern created is an ambiguous succession of POS tags or syntactic dependencies without any lexicalization. This suggests that, even when our classifier is incorrect, the rules decoded tend to capture the underlying semantics.

5 Conclusion

We introduced a strategy that jointly bootstraps a relation extraction classifier with a decoder that generates explanations for these extractions, using as sole supervision a set of example patterns that match such relations. Our experiments on the TACRED dataset demonstrated that our approach outperforms the strong rule-based method that provided the training patterns by 9 F1 points, while decoding explanations at over 90% BLEU score. Further, we showed that the joint training of the classification and explanation components performs better than training them separately. All in all, our work suggests that it is possible to marry the interpretability of rule-based methods with the performance of neural approaches.

[5]For this experiment we sorted the rules in descending order of their match frequency in training, and kept the top $n\%$ in each setting.

[6] The high BLEU score in the 20% configuration is due to the small sample in development for which gold rules exist.

References

Gabor Angeli, Victor Zhong, Danqi Chen, A. Chaganty, J. Bolton, Melvin Jose Johnson Premkumar, Panupong Pasupat, S. Gupta, and Christopher D. Manning. 2015. Bootstrapped self training for knowledge base population. *Theory and Applications of Categories*.

Douglas E Appelt, Jerry R Hobbs, John Bear, David Israel, and Mabry Tyson. 1993. Fastus: A finite-state processor for information extraction from real-world text. In *IJCAI*, volume 93, pages 1172–1178.

Razvan Bunescu and Raymond Mooney. 2005. A shortest path dependency kernel for relation extraction. In *Proceedings of Human Language Technology Conference and Conference on Empirical Methods in Natural Language Processing*, pages 724–731.

Nathanael Chambers, Daniel Cer, Trond Grenager, David Hall, Chloe Kiddon, Bill MacCartney, Marie-Catherine de Marneffe, Daniel Ramage, Eric Yeh, and Christopher D. Manning. 2007. Learning alignments and leveraging natural logic. In *Proceedings of the ACL-PASCAL Workshop on Textual Entailment and Paraphrasing*, pages 165–170, Prague. Association for Computational Linguistics.

Angel X Chang and Christopher D Manning. 2014. Tokensregex: Defining cascaded regular expressions over tokens. *Stanford University Computer Science Technical Reports. CSTR*, 2:2014.

Angel X Chang, Valentin I Spitkovsky, Eric Yeh, Eneko Agirre, and Christopher D Manning. 2010. Stanford-ubc entity linking at tac-kbp.

Laura Chiticariu, Yunyao Li, and Frederick Reiss. 2013. Rule-based information extraction is dead! long live rule-based information extraction systems! In *Proceedings of the 2013 conference on empirical methods in natural language processing*, pages 827–832.

Mark Craven and Jude W Shavlik. 1996. Extracting tree-structured representations of trained networks. In *Advances in neural information processing systems*, pages 24–30.

John Duchi, Elad Hazan, and Yoram Singer. 2011. Adaptive subgradient methods for online learning and stochastic optimization. *Journal of machine learning research*, 12(7).

Nicholas Frosst and Geoffrey Hinton. 2017. Distilling a neural network into a soft decision tree. *arXiv preprint arXiv:1711.09784*.

Zellig S Harris. 1954. Distributional structure. *Word*, 10(2-3):146–162.

Lisa Anne Hendricks, Zeynep Akata, Marcus Rohrbach, Jeff Donahue, Bernt Schiele, and Trevor Darrell. 2016. Generating visual explanations. In *European Conference on Computer Vision*, pages 3–19. Springer.

Sepp Hochreiter and Jürgen Schmidhuber. 1997. Long short-term memory. *Neural computation*, 9(8):1735–1780.

Sharmistha Jat, Siddhesh Khandelwal, and Partha Talukdar. 2018. Improving distantly supervised relation extraction using word and entity based attention. *arXiv preprint arXiv:1804.06987*.

Thomas N Kipf and Max Welling. 2016. Semi-supervised classification with graph convolutional networks. *arXiv preprint arXiv:1609.02907*.

Heeyoung Lee, Angel Chang, Yves Peirsman, Nathanael Chambers, Mihai Surdeanu, and Dan Jurafsky. 2013. Deterministic coreference resolution based on entity-centric, precision-ranked rules. *Computational Linguistics*, 39(4):885–916. Copyright: Copyright 2020 Elsevier B.V., All rights reserved.

Dekang Lin and P. Pantel. 2001. Dirt – discovery of inference rules from text.

Edward Loper and Steven Bird. 2002. Nltk: The natural language toolkit. In *In Proceedings of the ACL Workshop on Effective Tools and Methodologies for Teaching Natural Language Processing and Computational Linguistics. Philadelphia: Association for Computational Linguistics*.

Christopher D. Manning, Mihai Surdeanu, John Bauer, Jenny Finkel, Steven J. Bethard, and David McClosky. 2014. The Stanford CoreNLP natural language processing toolkit. In *Association for Computational Linguistics (ACL) System Demonstrations*, pages 55–60.

Mike Mintz, Steven Bills, Rion Snow, and Dan Jurafsky. 2009. Distant supervision for relation extraction without labeled data. In *Proceedings of the Joint Conference of the 47th Annual Meeting of the ACL and the 4th International Joint Conference on Natural Language Processing of the AFNLP*, pages 1003–1011.

Jeffrey Pennington, Richard Socher, and Christopher D Manning. 2014. Glove: Global vectors for word representation. In *Proceedings of the 2014 conference on empirical methods in natural language processing (EMNLP)*, pages 1532–1543.

Marco Tulio Ribeiro, Sameer Singh, and Carlos Guestrin. 2016. Why should i trust you?: Explaining the predictions of any classifier. In *Proceedings of the 22nd ACM SIGKDD international conference on knowledge discovery and data mining*, pages 1135–1144. ACM.

Ellen Riloff. 1996. Automatically generating extraction patterns from untagged text. In *Proceedings of the national conference on artificial intelligence*, pages 1044–1049.

Mihai Surdeanu, Julie Tibshirani, Ramesh Nallapati, and Christopher D. Manning. 2012. Multi-instance multi-label learning for relation extraction. In *Proceedings of the 2012 Joint Conference on Empirical Methods in Natural Language Processing and Computational Natural Language Learning*, pages 455–465, Jeju Island, Korea. Association for Computational Linguistics.

Marco A. Valenzuela-Escarcega, Ozgun Babur, Gus Hahn-Powell, Dane Bell, Thomas Hicks, Enrique Noriega-Atala, Xia Wang, Mihai Surdeanu, Emek Demir, and Clayton T. Morrison. 2018. Large-scale automated machine reading discovers new cancer driving mechanisms. *Database: The Journal of Biological Databases and Curation*.

Marco A. Valenzuela-Escárcega, Gus Hahn-Powell, and Mihai Surdeanu. 2016. Odin's runes: A rule language for information extraction. In *Proceedings of the Tenth International Conference on Language Resources and Evaluation (LREC'16)*, pages 322–329, Portorož, Slovenia. European Language Resources Association (ELRA).

Ngoc Thang Vu, Heike Adel, Pankaj Gupta, and Hinrich Schütze. 2016. Combining recurrent and convolutional neural networks for relation classification. In *Proceedings of the 2016 Conference of the North American Chapter of the Association for Computational Linguistics: Human Language Technologies*, pages 534–539, San Diego, California. Association for Computational Linguistics.

Linlin Wang, Zhu Cao, Gerard de Melo, and Zhiyuan Liu. 2016. Relation classification via multi-level attention CNNs. In *Proceedings of the 54th Annual Meeting of the Association for Computational Linguistics (Volume 1: Long Papers)*, pages 1298–1307, Berlin, Germany. Association for Computational Linguistics.

Yan Xu, Lili Mou, Ge Li, Yunchuan Chen, Hao Peng, and Zhi Jin. 2015. Classifying relations via long short term memory networks along shortest dependency paths. In *Proceedings of the 2015 Conference on Empirical Methods in Natural Language Processing*, pages 1785–1794, Lisbon, Portugal. Association for Computational Linguistics.

Dmitry Zelenko, Chinatsu Aone, and Anthony Richardella. 2003. Kernel methods for relation extraction. *Journal of machine learning research*, 3(Feb):1083–1106.

Daojian Zeng, Kang Liu, Siwei Lai, Guangyou Zhou, and Jun Zhao. 2014. Relation classification via convolutional deep neural network. In *Proceedings of COLING 2014, the 25th International Conference on Computational Linguistics: Technical Papers*, pages 2335–2344.

Dongxu Zhang and Dong Wang. 2015. Relation classification via recurrent neural network. *arXiv preprint arXiv:1508.01006*.

Yuhao Zhang, Peng Qi, and Christopher D. Manning. 2018. Graph convolution over pruned dependency trees improves relation extraction. In *Proceedings of the 2018 Conference on Empirical Methods in Natural Language Processing*, pages 2205–2215, Brussels, Belgium. Association for Computational Linguistics.

Yuhao Zhang, Victor Zhong, Danqi Chen, Gabor Angeli, and Christopher D. Manning. 2017. Position-aware attention and supervised data improve slot filling. In *Proceedings of the 2017 Conference on Empirical Methods in Natural Language Processing (EMNLP 2017)*, pages 35–45.

Peng Zhou, Wei Shi, Jun Tian, Zhenyu Qi, Bingchen Li, Hongwei Hao, and Bo Xu. 2016. Attention-based bidirectional long short-term memory networks for relation classification. In *Proceedings of the 54th Annual Meeting of the Association for Computational Linguistics (Volume 2: Short Papers)*, pages 207–212, Berlin, Germany. Association for Computational Linguistics.

A Experimental Details

We use the dependency parse trees, POS and NER sequences as included in the original release of the TACRED dataset, which was generated with Stanford CoreNLP (Manning et al., 2014). We use the pretrained 300-dimensional GloVe vectors (Pennington et al., 2014) to initialize word embeddings. We use a 2 layers of bi-LSTM, 2 layers of GCN, and 2 layers of feedforward in our encoder. And 2 layers of LSTM and 1 layer of feedforward in our decoder. Table 4 shows the details of the proposed neural network. We apply the ReLU function for all nonlinearities in the GCN layers and the standard max pooling operations in all pooling layers. For regularization we use dropout with p = 0.5 to all encoder LSTM layers and all but the last GCN layers.

For training, we use Adagrad (Duchi et al., 2011) an initial learning rate, and from epoch 1 we start to anneal the learning rate by a factor of 0.9 every time the F1 score on the development set does not increase after one epoch. We tuned the initial learning rate between 0.01 and 1; we chose 0.3 as this obtained the best performance on development. We trained 100 epochs for all the experiments with a batch size of 50. There were 3,850 positive data points and 12,311 negative data in the rule-only data. For this dataset, it took 1 minute to finish one epoch in average. And for Rules + TACRED training data, it took 4 minutes to finish one epoch in average[7].

Encoder and classifier components	Size
Vocabulary	53953
POS embedding dimension	30
NER embedding dimension	30
LSTM hidden layers	200
Feedforward layers	200
GCN layers	200
Relation	41
Decoder component	**Size**
LSTM hidden layers	200
Pattern embedding dimension	100
Feedforward layer	200
Maximum decoding length	100
Pattern	1141

Table 4: Details of our neural architecture.

All the hyperparameters above were tuned manually. We trained our model on PyTorch 3.8.5 with CUDA version 10.0, using one NVDIA Titan RTX.

B Dataset Introduction

You can find the details of TACRED data in this link: `https://nlp.stanford.edu/projects/tacred/`.

C Rules

The rule-base system we use is the combination of Stanford's Tokensregex (Chang and Manning, 2014) and Semregex (Chambers et al., 2007). The rules we use are from the system of Angeli et al. (2015), which contains 4528 Tokensregex patterns and 169 Semgrex patterns.

We extracted the rules from CoreNLP and mapped each rule to the TACRED dataset. We provided the mapping files in our released dataset. We also generate the dataset with only datapoints matched by rules in TACRED training partition and its mapping file.

[7]The software is available at this URL: https://github.com/clulab/releases/tree/master/naacl-trustnlp2021-edin.

Measuring Biases of Word Embeddings: What Similarity Measures and Descriptive Statistics to Use?

Hossein Azarpanah and **Mohsen Farhadloo**
John Molson School of Business
Concordia University
Montreal, QC, CA
(hossein.azarpanah, mohsen.farhadloo)@concordia.ca

Abstract

Word embeddings are widely used in Natural Language Processing (NLP) for a vast range of applications. However, it has been consistently proven that these embeddings reflect the same human biases that exist in the data used to train them. Most of the introduced bias indicators to reveal word embeddings' bias are average-based indicators based on the cosine similarity measure. In this study, we examine the impacts of different similarity measures as well as other descriptive techniques than averaging in measuring the biases of contextual and non-contextual word embeddings. We show that the extent of revealed biases in word embeddings depends on the descriptive statistics and similarity measures used to measure the bias. We found that over the ten categories of word embedding association tests, Mahalanobis distance reveals the smallest bias, and Euclidean distance reveals the largest bias in word embeddings. In addition, the contextual models reveal less severe biases than the non-contextual word embedding models with GPT showing the fewest number of WEAT biases.

1 Introduction

Word embedding models including *Word2Vec* (Mikolov et al., 2013), *GloVe* (Pennington et al., 2014), *BERT* (Devlin et al., 2018), *ELMo* (Peters et al., 2018), and *GPT* (Radford et al., 2018) have become popular components of many NLP frameworks and are vastly used for many downstream tasks. However, these word representations preserve not only statistical properties of human language but also the human-like biases that exist in the data used to train them (Bolukbasi et al., 2016; Caliskan et al., 2017; Kurita et al., 2019; Basta et al., 2019; Gonen and Goldberg, 2019). It has also been shown that such biases propagate to the downstream NLP tasks and have negative impacts on their performance (May et al., 2019; Leino et al., 2018). There are studies investigating how to mitigate biases of word embeddings (Liang et al., 2020; Ravfogel et al., 2020).

Different approaches have been used to present and quantify corpus-level biases of word embeddings. Bolukbasi et al. (2016) proposed to measure the gender bias of word representations in *Word2Vec* and *GloVe* by calculating the projections into principal components of differences of embeddings of a list of male and female pairs. Basta et al. (2019) adapted the idea of "gender direction" of (Bolukbasi et al., 2016) to be applicable to contextual word embeddings such as *ELMo*. In (Basta et al., 2019) first, the gender subspace of *ELMo* vector representations is calculated and then, the presence of gender bias in *ELMo* is identified. Gonen and Goldberg (2019) introduced a new gender bias indicator based on the percentage of socially-biased terms among the k-nearest neighbors of a target term and demonstrated its correlation with the gender direction indicator.

Caliskan et al. (2017) developed Word Embedding Association Test (WEAT) to measure bias by comparing two sets of target words with two sets of attribute words and documented that *Word2Vec* and *GloVe* contain human-like biases such as gender and racial biases. May et al. (2019) generalized the WEAT test to phrases and sentences by inserting individual words from WEAT tests into simple sentence templates and used them for contextual word embeddings.

Kurita et al. (2019) proposed a new method to quantify bias in *BERT* embeddings based on its masked language model objective using simple template sentences. For each attribute word, using a simple template sentence, the normalized probability that *BERT* assigns to that sentence for each of the target words is calculated, and the difference is considered the measure of the bias. Kurita et al. (2019) demonstrated that this probability-based method for quantifying bias in *BERT* was more effective than the cosine-based method.

Proceedings of the First Workshop on Trustworthy Natural Language Processing, pages 8–14

Motivated by these recent studies, we comprehensively investigate different methods for bias exposure in word embeddings. Particularly, we investigate the impacts of different similarity measures and descriptive statistics to demonstrate the degree of associations between the target sets and attribute sets in the WEAT. First, other than cosine similarity, we study Euclidean, Manhattan, and Mahalanobis distances to measure the degree of association between a single target word and a single attribute word. Second, other than averaging, we investigate minimum, maximum, median, and a discrete (grid-based) optimization approach to find the minimum possible association to report between a single target word and the two attribute sets in each of the WEAT tests. We consistently compare these bias measures for different types of word embeddings including non-contextual (*Word2Vec*, *GloVe*) and contextual ones (*BERT*, *ELMo*, *GPT*, *GPT2*).

2 Method

Implicit Association Test (IAT) was first introduced by Greenwald et al. (1998a) in psychology to demonstrate the enormous differences in response time when participants are asked to pair two concepts they deem similar, in contrast to two concepts they find less similar. For example, when subjects are encouraged to work as quickly as possible, they are much likely to label flowers as pleasant and insects as unpleasant. In IAT, being able to pair a concept to an attribute quickly indicates that the concept and attribute are linked together in the participants' minds. The IAT has widely been used to measure and quantify the strength of a range of implicit biases and other phenomena, including attitudes and stereotype threat (Karpinski and Hilton, 2001; Kiefer and Sekaquaptewa, 2007; Stanley et al., 2011).

Inspired by IAT, Caliskan et al. (2017) introduced WEAT to measure the associations between two sets of target concepts and two sets of attributes in word embeddings learned from large text corpora. A hypothesis test is conducted to demonstrate and quantify the bias. The null hypothesis states that there is no difference between the two sets of target words in terms of their relative distance/similarity to the two sets of attribute words. A permutation test is performed to measure the null hypothesis's likelihood. This test computes the probability that target words' random permutations would produce a greater difference than the observed difference. Let $\boldsymbol{X}$ and $\boldsymbol{Y}$ be two sets of target word embeddings and $\boldsymbol{A}$ and $\boldsymbol{B}$ be two sets of attribute embeddings. The test statistics is defined as:

$$s(\boldsymbol{X},\boldsymbol{Y},\boldsymbol{A},\boldsymbol{B}) = |\textstyle\sum_{x\in\boldsymbol{X}} s(x,\boldsymbol{A},\boldsymbol{B}) - \sum_{y\in\boldsymbol{Y}} s(y,\boldsymbol{A},\boldsymbol{B})|$$

where:

$$s(w,\boldsymbol{A},\boldsymbol{B}) = f_{a\in\boldsymbol{A}}(s(\overrightarrow{w},\overrightarrow{a})) - f_{b\in\boldsymbol{B}}(s(\overrightarrow{w},\overrightarrow{b})) \quad (1)$$

In other words, $s(w,\boldsymbol{A},\boldsymbol{B})$ quantifies the association of a single word w with the two sets of attributes, and $s(\boldsymbol{X},\boldsymbol{Y},\boldsymbol{A},\boldsymbol{B})$ measures the differential association of the two sets of targets with the two sets of attributes. Denoting all the partitions of $\boldsymbol{X}\cup\boldsymbol{Y}$ with $(\boldsymbol{X_i},\boldsymbol{Y_i})_i$, the one-sided p-value of the permutation test is:

$$Pr_i(s(\boldsymbol{X_i},\boldsymbol{Y_i},\boldsymbol{A},\boldsymbol{B}) > s(\boldsymbol{X},\boldsymbol{Y},\boldsymbol{A},\boldsymbol{B}))$$

The magnitude of the association of the two target sets with the two attribute sets can be measured with the effect size as:

$$d = \frac{|\overline{s(x,\boldsymbol{A},\boldsymbol{B})} - \overline{s(y,\boldsymbol{A},\boldsymbol{B})}|}{\text{std-dev}_{w\in\boldsymbol{X}\cup\boldsymbol{Y}}\, s(w,\boldsymbol{A},\boldsymbol{B})}$$

It is worth mentioning that d is a measure used to calculate how separated two distributions are and is basically the standardized difference of the means of the two distributions (Cohen, 2013). Controlling for the significance, a larger effect size reflects a more severe bias.

WEAT and almost all the other studies inspired by it (Garg et al., 2018; Brunet et al., 2018; Gonen and Goldberg, 2019; May et al., 2019) use the following approach to measure the association of a single target word with the two sets of attributes (equation 1). First, they use cosine similarity to measure the target word's similarity to each word in the attribute sets. Then they calculate the average of the similarities over each attribute set.

In this paper we investigate the impacts of other functions such as $min(\cdot)$, $mean(\cdot)$, $median(\cdot)$, or $max(\cdot)$ for function $f(\cdot)$ in equation (1) (originally only $mean(\cdot)$ has been used). Also, in this paper in addition to cosine similarity, we consider Euclidean and Manhattan distances as well as the following measures for the $s(\overrightarrow{w},\overrightarrow{a})$ in equation (1).

Mahalanobis distance: introduced by P. C. Mahalanobis (Mahalanobis, 1936) this distance measures the distance of a point from a distribution: $s(\overrightarrow{w},\overrightarrow{a}) = ((\overrightarrow{w} - \overrightarrow{a})^T\Sigma_A^{-1}(\overrightarrow{w} - \overrightarrow{a}))^{\frac{1}{2}}$. It is worth noting that the Mahalanobis distance takes into account the distribution of the set of attributes while measuring the association of the target word w with an attribute vector.

Discrete optimization of the association measure: In equation (1), $s(w, \boldsymbol{A}, \boldsymbol{B})$ quantifies the association of a single target word w with the two sets of attributes. To quantify the minimum possible association of a target word w with the two sets of attributes, we first calculate the distance of w from all attribute words in $\boldsymbol{A}$ and $\boldsymbol{B}$, then calculate all possible differences and find the minimum difference.

$$s(w, \boldsymbol{A}, \boldsymbol{B}) = \min_{a \in \boldsymbol{A}, b \in \boldsymbol{B}} |s(\vec{w}, \vec{a}) - s(\vec{w}, \vec{b})| \quad (2)$$

3 Biases studied

We studied all ten bias categories introduced in IAT (Greenwald et al., 1998a) and replicated in WEAT to measure the biases in word embeddings. The ten WEAT categories are briefly introduced in Table 1. For more detail and example of target and attribute words, please check Appendix A. Although WEAT 3 to 5 have the same names, they have different target and attribute words.

WEAT	Association
1	Flowers vs insects with pleasant vs unpleasant
2	Instruments vs weapons with pleasant vs unpleasant
3	Eur.-American vs Afr.-American names with Pleasant vs unpleasant (Greenwald et al., 1998b)
4	Eur.-American vs Afr.-American names (Bertrand and Mullainathan, 2004) with Pleasant vs unpleasant (Greenwald et al., 1998b)
5	Eur.-American vs Afr.-American names (Bertrand and Mullainathan, 2004) with Pleasant vs unpleasant (Nosek et al., 2002)
6	Male vs female names with Career vs family
7	Math vs arts with male vs female terms
8	Science vs arts with male vs female terms
9	Mental vs physical disease with temporary vs permanent
10	Young vs old people's name with pleasant vs unpleasant

Table 1: The associations studied in the WEAT

As described in section 2, we need each attribute set's covariance matrix to compute Mahalanobis distance. To get stable covariance matrix estimation due to the high dimension of the embeddings we first created larger attribute sets by adding synonym terms. Next, we estimated the sparse covariance matrices as the number of samples in each attribute set is smaller than the number of features. To enforce sparsity, we estimated the $l1$ penalty using k-fold cross validation with k=3.

4 Results of experiments

We examined the 10 different types of biases in WEAT (Table 1) for word embedding models listed in Table 2. We used publicly available pre-trained models. For contextual word embeddings, we used single word sentences as input instead of using simple template sentences used in other studies (May et al., 2019; Kurita et al., 2019). The simple template sentences such as "this is TARGET" or "TARGET is ATTRIBUTE" used in other studies do not really provide any context to reveal the contextual capability of embeddings such as *BERT* or *ELMo*. This way, the comparisons between the contextual embeddings and non-contextual embeddings are fairer as both of them only get the target or attribute terms as input. For each model, we performed the WEAT tests using four similarity metrics mentioned in section 2: *cosine, Euclidean, Manhattan, Mahalanobis*. For each similarity metric, we also used $min(\cdot)$, $mean(\cdot)$, $median(\cdot)$, or $max(\cdot)$ as the $f(\cdot)$ in equation (1). Also, as explained in section 2, we discretely optimized the association measure and found the minimum association in equation (1). In these experiments (Table 3 and Table 4), the larger and more significant effect sizes imply more severe biases.

Model	Embedding	Dim
GloVe (840B tokens, web corpus)	-	300
Word2Vec (GoogleNews-negative)	-	300
ELMo (original)	First hidden layer	1024
BERT (base, cased)	Sum of last 4 hidden layers in [CLS]	768
GPT	Last hidden layer	768
GPT2	Last hidden layer	768

Table 2: Word embedding models, used representations, and their dimensions.

Impacts of different descriptive statistics: Our first goal was to report the changes in the measured biases when we change the descriptive statistics. The range of effect sizes was from 0.00 to 1.89 ($\mu = 0.65$, $\sigma = 0.5$). Our findings show that *mean* has a better capability to reveal biases as it provides the most cases of significant effect sizes ($\mu = 0.8$, $\sigma = 0.52$) across models and distance measures. *Median* is close to the *mean* with ($\mu = 0.74$, $\sigma = 0.48$) among all its effect sizes. The effect sizes for *minimum* ($\mu = 0.68$, $\sigma = 0.48$) and *maximum* ($\mu = 0.65$, $\sigma = 0.48$) are close to each other, but smaller than *mean* and *median*. The discretely optimized association measure (Eq. 2) provides the smallest effect sizes ($\mu = 0.39$, $\sigma = 0.3$) and reveals the least number of implicit biases. These differences as the result of applying different descriptive statistics in the association measure (Eq. (1)) show that the revealed biases depend on the applied statistics to measure the bias.

For example, in the *cosine* distance of *Word2Vec*, if we change the descriptive statistic from *mean* to *minimum*, the biases for WEAT 3 and WEAT 4 will become insignificant (no bias will be reported). In another example, in *GPT* model, while the result of *mean cosine* is not significant for WEAT 3 and WEAT 4, they become significant for *median cosine*. Moreover, almost for all models, the effect size of the discretely optimized minimum distance is not significant. Our intention for considering this statistic was to report the minimum possible association of a target word with the attribute sets. If this measure is used for reporting biases, one can misleadingly claim that there is no bias.

Impacts of different similarity measures: The effect sizes for cosine, Manhattan, and Euclidean are closer to each other and greater than the Mahalanobis distance (cosine: ($\mu = 0.72, \sigma = 0.49$), Euclidean: ($\mu = 0.67$, $\sigma = 0.5$), Manhattan: ($\mu = 0.63, \sigma = 0.48$), Mahalanobis: ($\mu = 0.58$, $\sigma = 0.45$)). Mahalanobis distance also detects the fewest number of significant bias types across all models. As an example, while *mean* and *median* effect sizes for WEAT 3 and WEAT 5 in *GloVe* and *Word2Vec* are mostly significant for *cosine, Euclidean, and Manhattan*; the same results are not significant for the *Mahalanobis* distance. That means with the Mahalanobis distance as the measure of the bias, no bias will be reported for WEAT 3 and WEAT 5 tests. This emphasizes the importance of chosen similarity measures in detecting biases of word embeddings. More importantly, as the *Mahalanobis* distance considers the distribution of attributes in measuring the distance, it may be a better choice than the other similarity measures for measuring and revealing biases with GPT showing fewer number of biases.

Biases in different word embedding models: Using any combination of descriptive statistics and similarity measures, all the contextualized models have less significant biases than *GloVe* and *Word2Vec*. In Table 3 the number of tests with significant implicit biases out of the 10 WEAT tests along with the mean and standard deviation of the effect sizes for all embedding models have been reported. The complete list of effect sizes along with their p-value are provided in Table 4.

Following our findings in the previous sections, we choose *mean* of Euclidean to reveal biases. By doing so, *GloVe* and *Word2Vec* show the most number of significant biases with 9 and 7 significant biases in 10 WEAT categories (Table 3). Using *mean of Euclidean*, our results confirm all the results by Caliskan et al. (2017), which used *mean of cosine* in all WEAT tests. The difference is that with the *mean of Euclidean* measure, the biases are revealed as being more severe. (smaller p-values). Using *mean* of Euclidean, *GPT* and *ELMo* show the fewest number of implicit biases. *GPT* model shows bias in WEAT 2, 3, and 5. *ELMo's* significant biases are in WEAT 1, 3, and 6. Using *mean Euclidean*, almost all models (except for *ELMo*) confirm the existence of a bias in WEAT 3 to 5. Moreover, all contextualized models found no bias in associating female with arts and male with science (WEAT 7), mental diseases with temporary attributes and physical diseases with permanent attributes (WEAT 9), and young people's name with pleasant attribute and old people's name with unpleasant attributes (WEAT 10).

Model	*mean cosine*	*mean Euc*	*mean Maha*	*Maha Eq.2*
GloVe	9 (1.39, 0.21)	9 (1.41, 0.2)	3 (0.79, 0.53)	0 (0.34, 0.27)
Word2Vec	7 (1.13, 0.54)	7 (1.13, 0.55)	5 (0.84, 0.52)	0 (0.32, 0.33)
ELMo	3 (0.64, 0.51)	3 (0,65, 0.52)	3 (0.61, 0.42)	0 (0.36, 0.23)
BERT	5 (0.74, 0.5)	5 (0.74, 0.48)	2 (0.47, 0.5)	2 (0.55, 0.52)
GPT	2 (0.61, 0.48)	3 (0.65, 0.42)	4 (0.59, 0.35)	0 (0.29, 0.27)
GPT2	3 (0.73, 0.46)	4 (0.71, 0.46)	3 (0.69, 0.49)	3 (0.66, 0.49)

Table 3: Number of revealed biases out of the 10 WEAT bias types for the studied word embeddings along with the (μ, σ) of their effect sizes. The larger the effect size the more severe the bias.

5 Conclusions

We studied the impacts of different descriptive statistics and similarity measures on association tests for measuring biases in contextualized and non-contextualized word embeddings. Our findings demonstrate that the detected biases depend on the choice of association measure. Based on our experiments, *mean* reveals more severe biases and the discretely optimized version reveals fewer number of severe biases. In addition, *cosine* distance reveals more severe biases and the *Mahalanobis* distance reveals less severe ones. Reporting biases with mean of Euclidean/Mahalanobis distances identifies more/less severe biases in the models. Furthermore, contextual models show less biases than the non-contextual ones across all 10 WEAT tests with GPT showing the fewest number of biases.

		Cosine					Euclidean					Manhattan					Mahalanobis				
Model	**WEAT**	**Mean**	**Median**	**Min**	**Max**	**Eq.2**	**Mean**	**Median**	**Min**	**Max**	**Eq.2**	**Mean**	**Median**	**Min**	**Max**	**Eq.2**	**Mean**	**Median**	**Min**	**Max**	**Eq.2**
GloVe	1	1.50^{****}	1.34^{****}	1.35^{***}	1.41^{****}	0.27	1.52^{****}	1.47^{****}	1.31^{****}	1.23^{****}	0.03	1.50^{****}	1.46^{****}	1.32^{****}	0.90^{**}	0.15	1.53^{****}	1.54^{****}	1.19^{****}	1.61^{****}	0.00
	2	1.53^{****}	1.37^{****}	0.83^{*}	1.57^{****}	0.08	1.53^{****}	1.42^{****}	1.42^{****}	0.03	0.13	1.51^{****}	1.43^{****}	1.44^{****}	0.27	0.24	1.61^{****}	1.63^{****}	1.49^{****}	0.98^{***}	0.28
	3	1.41^{****}	1.13^{****}	1.53^{****}	1.41^{****}	0.60^{*}	1.37^{****}	0.98^{****}	1.51^{****}	0.09	0.31	0.82^{**}	0.37	1.24^{****}	0.69^{*}	0.21	0.57	0.66^{*}	0.37	0.89^{**}	0.13
	4	1.50^{****}	1.02^{*}	1.55^{****}	1.47^{****}	0.17	1.51^{****}	0.40	1.58^{****}	0.32	0.06	0.93^{*}	0.36	1.14^{***}	0.80^{*}	0.05	0.30	0.57	0.04	0.67	0.31
	5	1.28^{***}	1.39^{***}	0.45	1.29^{***}	0.57	1.30^{****}	1.62^{****}	1.13^{**}	0.36	0.61	0.54	1.03^{*}	0.17	0.11	0.37	0.17	0.36	0.01	0.69	0.35
	6	1.81^{***}	1.83^{***}	1.70^{***}	1.67^{***}	1.01	1.80^{****}	1.75^{****}	1.75^{****}	1.56^{***}	0.17	1.78^{****}	1.78^{****}	1.71^{****}	1.46^{**}	0.86	1.17^{*}	0.83	1.27^{*}	0.60	0.43
	7	1.06	0.85	0.61	1.05	0.18	1.10	0.65	0.26	0.70	0.16	0.70	0.03	0.55	0.63	0.50	0.20	0.80	0.02	0.23	0.10
	8	1.24^{*}	0.93	1.29^{*}	1.16^{*}	0.36	1.23^{*}	1.07	1.12	0.92	0.21	1.03	0.81	0.99	0.83	0.13	0.92	0.71	0.86	0.26	0.26
	9	1.38^{*}	0.83	0.37	1.47^{*}	1.03	1.47^{*}	1.04	1.20	1.32^{*}	0.90	1.50^{*}	0.26	1.18	1.42^{*}	0.61	0.99	0.93	1.20	0.55	0.85
	10	1.21^{*}	1.05	1.01	0.75	0.99	1.26^{*}	1.42^{*}	0.84	0.64	0.41	0.70	0.90	0.34	0.46	0.25	0.47	0.83	0.45	0.60	0.71
word2vec	1	1.54^{****}	1.34^{****}	0.55	1.49^{****}	0.16	1.50^{****}	1.30^{****}	1.31^{****}	0.95^{**}	0.31	1.49^{****}	1.34^{****}	1.38^{****}	0.75^{*}	0.26	0.84^{*}	1.06^{***}	0.79^{*}	0.34	0.13
	2	1.63^{****}	1.49^{****}	1.19^{****}	1.60^{****}	0.22	1.58^{****}	1.36^{****}	1.37^{****}	0.68^{*}	0.10	1.44^{****}	1.24^{****}	1.19^{****}	0.70^{*}	0.36	1.39^{****}	0.99^{***}	0.39	0.15	0.05
	3	0.58^{*}	0.46	0.10	0.81^{**}	0.38	0.78^{**}	0.46	0.82^{**}	0.62^{*}	0.19	0.82^{**}	0.56	0.68^{*}	0.63^{*}	0.17	0.24	0.41	0.98^{****}	0.68^{*}	0.19
	4	1.31^{****}	1.21^{***}	0.44	1.27^{****}	0.09	1.49^{****}	0.80^{*}	1.66^{****}	0.60	0.35	1.44^{****}	1.13^{***}	1.37^{***}	0.55	0.86^{*}	0.55	0.16	1.30^{****}	0.49	0.28
	5	0.72	0.68	0.58	0.41	0.19	0.43	0.38	0.41	0.08	0.25	0.27	0.23	0.11	0.05	0.09	0.02	0.61	0.11	0.12	0.24
	6	1.89^{***}	1.87^{***}	1.76^{***}	1.65^{***}	0.91	1.88^{****}	1.88^{****}	1.63^{**}	1.70^{****}	0.85	1.89^{****}	1.87^{****}	1.39^{*}	1.76^{****}	0.39	1.21^{*}	0.24	1.49^{**}	0.29	0.01
	7	0.97	0.98	0.52	0.71	0.67	0.92	0.45	1.11^{*}	1.27^{*}	0.70	1.06	0.87	1.04	1.27^{*}	1.29^{*}	0.97	0.90	0.55	1.35^{*}	0.08
	8	1.24^{*}	1.23^{*}	1.18^{*}	0.99	0.59	1.25^{*}	1.09	1.21^{*}	1.49^{**}	0.60	1.47^{*}	1.36^{*}	1.33^{*}	1.67^{***}	0.00	0.40	0.30	0.48	0.52	0.88
	9	1.30^{*}	0.69	0.14	1.31	0.42	1.32^{*}	1.18	1.07	0.92	0.55	1.08	0.92	0.92	0.46	0.09	1.55^{****}	1.23	0.59	0.41	0.94
	10	0.09	0.01	0.19	0.66	0.76	0.15	0.01	0.39	0.14	0.43	0.24	0.12	0.36	0.34	0.05	1.20^{*}	1.24^{*}	1.60^{***}	0.03	0.44
ELMo	1	1.25^{****}	1.15^{***}	0.77^{*}	0.68^{*}	0.03	1.25^{****}	1.03^{***}	0.51	0.35	0.48	1.24^{****}	1.04^{***}	0.50	0.27	0.19	0.28	0.17	0.28	0.26	0.57
	2	1.46^{****}	1.37^{****}	0.87^{**}	1.37^{****}	0.08	1.46^{****}	1.28^{****}	1.14^{****}	0.71^{*}	0.51	1.50^{****}	1.22^{****}	1.25^{****}	0.75^{*}	0.27	0.67^{*}	0.11	0.79^{*}	0.11	0.15
	3	0.19	0.19	0.06	0.10	0.30	0.12	0.30	0.20	0.06	0.14	0.16	0.02	0.15	0.12	0.19	0.24	0.29	0.37	0.07	0.27
	4	0.29	0.22	0.66	0.44	0.02	0.39	0.07	0.03	0.35	0.19	0.39	0.00	0.02	0.35	0.34	0.33	0.29	0.25	0.08	0.48
	5	0.11	0.01	0.27	0.57	0.43	0.14	0.12	0.46	0.14	0.09	0.03	0.04	0.55	0.20	0.85^{*}	0.40	0.04	0.71	0.52	0.34
	6	1.24^{*}	0.95	0.61	0.10	1.00	1.27^{*}	0.50	0.02	0.44	0.53	0.30	0.59	0.51	0.20	0.49	1.34^{*}	1.10	0.06	0.50	0.22
	7	0.32	0.30	0.56	0.25	0.81	0.29	0.48	0.02	0.62	0.81	0.24	0.25	0.41	0.36	0.03	1.34^{*}	1.49^{**}	0.72	0.95	0.88
	8	0.28	0.42	0.00	0.38	0.29	0.37	0.14	0.14	0.86	0.66	0.64	0.38	0.61	0.99	0.35	0.18	1.06	0.15	0.06	0.15
	9	0.91	0.24	0.67	1.28^{*}	0.68	0.93	0.59	1.04	0.69	0.10	1.06	0.65	0.98	0.77	0.38	0.71	0.55	0.94	0.23	0.38
	10	0.37	0.81	0.53	0.56	0.23	0.33	0.93	0.36	0.13	0.62	0.28	0.74	0.49	0.06	0.62	0.61	0.73	0.26	0.48	0.20
BERT	1	0.00	0.21	0.12	0.05	0.72^{*}	0.01	0.21	0.09	0.11	0.18	0.02	0.32	0.05	0.18	0.46	0.10	0.11	0.24	0.27	0.06
	2	0.62	0.39	0.90^{**}	0.55	0.32	0.63	0.45	0.56	1.02^{**}	0.24	0.58	0.45	0.23	0.79^{*}	0.27	1.31^{****}	1.33^{****}	1.35^{****}	1.25^{****}	1.21^{****}
	3	1.04^{***}	1.02^{***}	0.75^{*}	0.83^{**}	0.58^{*}	1.05^{****}	1.07^{****}	0.77^{**}	0.72^{*}	0.21	1.04^{****}	1.09^{****}	0.82^{**}	0.76^{**}	0.01	0.24	0.30	0.23	0.29	0.17
	4	1.19^{***}	1.19^{***}	1.06^{***}	1.08^{**}	0.26	1.23^{***}	0.97^{*}	1.00^{**}	1.16^{****}	0.65	1.20^{***}	1.07^{**}	0.88^{*}	1.10^{***}	0.13	0.27	0.31	0.44	0.17	0.05
	5	0.94^{*}	0.93^{*}	0.30	0.77^{*}	0.06	0.88^{*}	0.95^{*}	0.58	0.11	0.41	0.85^{*}	0.98^{*}	0.71	0.02	0.45	0.29	0.23	0.04	0.34	0.19
	6	1.36^{*}	1.20^{*}	1.32^{*}	0.13	0.22	1.30^{*}	1.15^{*}	0.20	1.45^{**}	0.96	1.12	0.83	0.16	1.34^{*}	0.82	0.03	0.15	0.24	0.61	0.38
	7	1.14^{*}	0.85	0.75	1.01	0.07	1.18^{*}	0.75	1.03	0.95^{*}	0.40	1.20^{*}	0.90	1.09	1.02^{*}	0.85	0.29	0.09	0.49	0.18	0.77
	8	0.24	0.37	0.11	0.55	0.17	0.24	0.02	0.50	0.73	0.37	0.12	0.14	0.13	0.34	0.04	0.47	0.42	0.61	0.27	0.60
	9	0.02	0.16	0.03	1.04	0.69	0.12	0.32	0.97	0.00	0.25	0.17	0.34	0.72	0.16	0.66	1.48^{*}	1.38^{*}	1.52^{*}	1.54^{*}	1.61^{*}
	10	0.83	0.76	0.89	0.50	1.28^{*}	0.80	0.89	0.40	0.90	0.22	0.91	1.16^{*}	0.57	0.72	0.53	0.24	0.28	0.09	0.54	0.47
GPT	1	0.47	0.29	0.57	0.08	0.24	0.58	0.39	0.10	0.10	0.50	0.57	0.25	0.11	0.01	0.10	0.40	0.00	0.54	0.45	0.13
	2	1.11^{***}	0.99^{**}	0.94^{**}	0.53	0.38	1.15^{****}	0.74^{*}	0.13	0.23	0.01	1.16^{****}	0.82^{*}	0.01	0.16	0.28	0.84^{**}	0.69^{*}	0.06	1.01^{**}	0.05
	3	0.09	0.97^{***}	0.64^{*}	1.24^{****}	0.20	0.70^{*}	0.99^{***}	1.21^{****}	0.27	0.02	0.06	1.05^{****}	1.17^{****}	0.56	0.01	0.69^{*}	0.97^{***}	1.24^{****}	0.90^{***}	0.13
	4	0.33	1.54^{****}	0.88^{*}	1.48^{****}	0.30	0.51	1.51^{****}	1.37^{****}	0.28	0.10	0.31	1.52^{****}	1.33^{****}	0.50	0.29	0.91^{**}	1.36^{****}	1.26^{***}	1.07^{***}	0.42
	5	1.65^{****}	1.40^{****}	1.57^{****}	1.58^{****}	0.69	1.57^{****}	1.14^{****}	1.49^{****}	1.65^{****}	0.26	1.54^{****}	1.23^{****}	1.49^{****}	1.50^{****}	0.57	1.26^{****}	1.23^{****}	0.98^{***}	1.40^{****}	0.06
	6	0.67	0.02	0.75	0.89	0.20	0.50	0.25	0.23	0.66	0.08	0.49	0.04	0.34	0.45	0.09	0.66	0.01	1.14^{*}	0.27	0.19
	7	0.24	0.11	0.02	0.09	0.70	0.20	0.30	0.00	0.15	0.45	0.28	0.16	0.32	0.03	0.18	0.29	0.63	0.22	0.57	0.06
	8	0.10	0.16	0.35	0.13	0.40	0.08	0.10	0.32	0.03	0.93^{*}	0.12	0.14	0.37	0.08	0.47	0.19	0.13	0.22	0.58	0.43
	9	0.70	0.92	1.01	0.01	0.18	0.58	0.63	0.17	0.07	0.42	0.59	0.62	0.40	0.01	0.44	0.50	0.59	0.66	0.03	0.62
	10	0.72	0.39	0.73	0.68	0.67	0.61	0.25	0.55	1.03	0.27	0.52	0.34	0.48	0.76	0.77	0.19	0.17	0.07	0.27	0.81
GPT2	1	0.11	0.06	0.20	0.20	0.19	0.06	0.21	0.14	0.04	0.01	0.08	0.05	0.05	0.07	0.04	0.27	0.27	0.26	0.23	0.28
	2	0.64	0.28	0.50	0.24	0.04	0.51	0.63	0.21	0.61^{*}	0.02	0.47	0.69^{*}	0.18	0.53	0.56	0.44	0.45	0.45	0.41	0.34
	3	1.27^{****}	0.70^{*}	1.07^{****}	1.15^{****}	0.30	1.25^{****}	1.21^{****}	0.29	1.30^{****}	0.48	1.34^{****}	1.24^{****}	0.39	1.12^{****}	0.11	1.25^{****}	1.25^{****}	1.27^{****}	1.22^{****}	1.24^{****}
	4	1.19^{**}	0.64	1.28^{***}	0.83^{*}	0.56	1.17^{***}	1.24^{****}	0.39	1.13^{**}	0.57	1.17^{***}	1.10^{**}	0.28	1.05^{**}	0.44	1.29^{****}	1.29^{****}	1.28^{****}	1.28^{***}	1.31^{****}
	5	1.17^{**}	1.15^{**}	1.31^{***}	1.02^{**}	0.06	1.17^{***}	1.21^{****}	0.92^{*}	1.13^{**}	0.77^{*}	1.14^{**}	1.18^{***}	0.13	1.15^{**}	0.42	1.29^{***}	1.29^{****}	1.28^{****}	1.30^{****}	1.29^{****}
	6	0.79	1.06	0.94	0.11	0.20	0.86	0.90	0.28	0.94	0.54	0.66	0.74	0.19	0.11	0.63	0.94	0.55	0.52	0.89	0.71
	7	0.03	0.49	0.21	0.69	0.17	0.12	0.10	0.24	0.00	0.07	0.23	0.42	0.34	0.01	0.16	0.16	0.17	0.16	0.16	0.14
	8	0.42	1.08	0.79	0.42	0.36	0.44	0.37	0.08	0.59	0.32	0.30	0.78	0.22	0.21	0.23	0.36	0.35	0.36	0.37	0.38
	9	0.57	0.68	0.16	0.17	0.73	0.36	0.41	0.39	0.64	0.24	0.04	0.10	1.19	0.32	0.05	0.06	0.05	0.14	0.21	0.04
	10	1.14	1.12	0.77	0.63	0.03	1.13^{*}	1.11	0.09	1.12	0.14	1.12	1.12	0.24	1.13	0.71	0.80	0.83	0.82	0.65	0.86

Table 4: WEAT effect size, *: significance at 0.01, **: significance at 0.001, ***: significance at 0.0001, ****: significance at 0.00001.

References

Christine Basta, Marta R Costa-jussà, and Noe Casas. 2019. Evaluating the underlying gender bias in contextualized word embeddings. *arXiv preprint arXiv:1904.08783*.

Marianne Bertrand and Sendhil Mullainathan. 2004. Are emily and greg more employable than lakisha and jamal? a field experiment on labor market discrimination. *American economic review*, 94(4):991–1013.

Tolga Bolukbasi, Kai-Wei Chang, James Y Zou, Venkatesh Saligrama, and Adam T Kalai. 2016. Man is to computer programmer as woman is to homemaker? debiasing word embeddings. In *Advances in neural information processing systems*, pages 4349–4357.

Marc-Etienne Brunet, Colleen Alkalay-Houlihan, Ashton Anderson, and Richard Zemel. 2018. Understanding the origins of bias in word embeddings. *arXiv preprint arXiv:1810.03611*.

Aylin Caliskan, Joanna J Bryson, and Arvind Narayanan. 2017. Semantics derived automatically from language corpora contain human-like biases. *Science*, 356(6334):183–186.

Jacob Cohen. 2013. *Statistical power analysis for the behavioral sciences*. Academic press.

Jacob Devlin, Ming-Wei Chang, Kenton Lee, and Kristina Toutanova. 2018. Bert: Pre-training of deep bidirectional transformers for language understanding. *arXiv preprint arXiv:1810.04805*.

Nikhil Garg, Londa Schiebinger, Dan Jurafsky, and James Zou. 2018. Word embeddings quantify 100 years of gender and ethnic stereotypes. *Proceedings of the National Academy of Sciences*, 115(16):E3635–E3644.

Hila Gonen and Yoav Goldberg. 2019. Lipstick on a pig: Debiasing methods cover up systematic gender biases in word embeddings but do not remove them. *arXiv preprint arXiv:1903.03862*.

Anthony G Greenwald, Debbie E McGhee, and Jordan LK Schwartz. 1998a. Measuring individual differences in implicit cognition: the implicit association test. *Journal of personality and social psychology*, 74(6):1464.

Anthony G Greenwald, Debbie E McGhee, and Jordan LK Schwartz. 1998b. Measuring individual differences in implicit cognition: the implicit association test. *Journal of personality and social psychology*, 74(6):1464.

Andrew Karpinski and James L Hilton. 2001. Attitudes and the implicit association test. *Journal of personality and social psychology*, 81(5):774.

Amy K Kiefer and Denise Sekaquaptewa. 2007. Implicit stereotypes and women's math performance: How implicit gender-math stereotypes influence women's susceptibility to stereotype threat. *Journal of experimental social psychology*, 43(5):825–832.

Keita Kurita, Nidhi Vyas, Ayush Pareek, Alan W Black, and Yulia Tsvetkov. 2019. Measuring bias in contextualized word representations. *arXiv preprint arXiv:1906.07337*.

Klas Leino, Emily Black, Matt Fredrikson, Shayak Sen, and Anupam Datta. 2018. Feature-wise bias amplification. *arXiv preprint arXiv:1812.08999*.

Paul Pu Liang, Irene Mengze Li, Emily Zheng, Yao Chong Lim, Ruslan Salakhutdinov, and Louis-Philippe Morency. 2020. Towards debiasing sentence representations. *arXiv preprint arXiv:2007.08100*.

Prasanta Chandra Mahalanobis. 1936. On the generalized distance in statitics. *Proceedings of the National Institute of Sciences of India*, pages 49–55.

Chandler May, Alex Wang, Shikha Bordia, Samuel R Bowman, and Rachel Rudinger. 2019. On measuring social biases in sentence encoders. *arXiv preprint arXiv:1903.10561*.

Tomas Mikolov, Ilya Sutskever, Kai Chen, Greg S Corrado, and Jeff Dean. 2013. Distributed representations of words and phrases and their compositionality. In *Advances in neural information processing systems*, pages 3111–3119.

Brian A Nosek, Mahzarin R Banaji, and Anthony G Greenwald. 2002. Harvesting implicit group attitudes and beliefs from a demonstration web site. *Group Dynamics: Theory, Research, and Practice*, 6(1):101.

Jeffrey Pennington, Richard Socher, and Christopher D Manning. 2014. Glove: Global vectors for word representation. In *Proceedings of the 2014 conference on empirical methods in natural language processing (EMNLP)*, pages 1532–1543.

Matthew E Peters, Mark Neumann, Mohit Iyyer, Matt Gardner, Christopher Clark, Kenton Lee, and Luke Zettlemoyer. 2018. Deep contextualized word representations. *arXiv preprint arXiv:1802.05365*.

Alec Radford, Karthik Narasimhan, Tim Salimans, and Ilya Sutskever. 2018. Improving language understanding by generative pre-training.

Shauli Ravfogel, Yanai Elazar, Hila Gonen, Michael Twiton, and Yoav Goldberg. 2020. Null it out: Guarding protected attributes by iterative nullspace projection. *arXiv preprint arXiv:2004.07667*.

Damian A Stanley, Peter Sokol-Hessner, Mahzarin R Banaji, and Elizabeth A Phelps. 2011. Implicit race attitudes predict trustworthiness judgments and economic trust decisions. *Proceedings of the National Academy of Sciences*, 108(19):7710–7715.

A The studied associations: 10 WEAT categories

WEAT	Association	N_T	N_A
1	Flowers vs insects with pleasant vs unpleasant Example: {aster, clover} vs {ant, caterpillar} with {caress, freedom} vs { abuse, crash}	25×2	25×2
2	Instruments vs weapons with pleasant vs unpleasant Example: {bagpipe, cello} vs {arrow, club} with {caress, freedom} vs { abuse, crash}	25×2	25×2
3	Eur.-American vs Afr.-American names with Pleasant vs unpleasant Example: {Adam, Harry} vs {Alonzo, Jamel} with {caress, freedom} vs {abuse, crash}	32×2	25×2
4	Eur.-American vs Afr.-American names with Pleasant vs unpleasant Example: {Brad, Brendan} vs {Darnell, Hakim} with {caress, freedom} vs {abuse, crash}	16×2	25×2
5	Eur.-American vs Afr.-American names with Pleasant vs unpleasant Example: {Brad, Brendan} vs {Darnell, Hakim} with {joy, love} vs {agony, terrible}	16×2	8×2
6	Male vs female names with Career vs family Example: {John, Paul} vs {Amy, Joan} with {executive, management} vs {home, parents}	8×2	8×2
7	Math vs arts with male vs female terms Example: {math, algebra} vs {poetry, art} with {male, man} vs {female, woman}	8×2	8×2
8	Science vs arts with male vs female terms Example: {science, technology} vs {art, Shakespeare} with {brother, father} vs {sister, mother}	8×2	8×2
9	Mental vs physical disease with temporary vs permanent Example: {sad, hopeless} vs {sick, illness} with {impermanent, unstable} vs {stable, always}	6×2	7×2
10	Young vs old people's name with pleasant vs unpleasant Example: {Tiffany, Michelle} vs {Ethel, Bernice} with {love, peace} vs {agony, terrible}	8×2	8×2

Table 1: The 10 WEAT categories.

Private Release of Text Embedding Vectors

Oluwaseyi Feyisetan
Amazon
Seattle, WA, USA
sey@amazon.com

Shiva Kasiviswanathan
Amazon
Palo Alto, CA, USA
kasivisw@amazon.com

Abstract

Ensuring strong theoretical privacy guarantees on text data is a challenging problem which is usually attained at the expense of utility. However, to improve the practicality of privacy preserving text analyses, it is essential to design algorithms that better optimize this tradeoff. To address this challenge, we propose a release mechanism that takes any (text) embedding vector as input and releases a corresponding private vector. The mechanism satisfies an extension of differential privacy to metric spaces. Our idea based on first randomly projecting the vectors to a lower-dimensional space and then adding noise in this projected space generates private vectors that achieve strong theoretical guarantees on its utility. We support our theoretical proofs with empirical experiments on multiple word embedding models and NLP datasets, achieving in some cases more than 10% gains over the existing state-of-the-art privatization techniques.

1 Introduction

Privacy has emerged as a topic of strategic consequence across all computational fields. Differential Privacy (DP) is a mathematical definition of privacy proposed by (Dwork et al., 2006). Ever since its introduction, DP has been widely adopted and as of today, it has become the *de facto* privacy definition in the academic world with also wide adoption in industry, e.g., (Erlingsson et al., 2014; Dajani et al., 2017; Team, 2017; Uber Security, 2017). DP provides provable protection against adversaries with arbitrary side information and computational power, allows clear quantification of privacy losses, and satisfies graceful composition over multiple access to the same data. In DP, two parameters ϵ and δ control the level of privacy. Very roughly, ϵ is an upper bound on the amount of influence a single data point has on the information released and δ is the probability that this bound fails to hold, so the definition becomes more stringent as $\epsilon, \delta \to 0$. The definition with $\delta = 0$ is referred to as *pure differential privacy*, and with $\delta > 0$ is referred to as *approximate differential privacy*.

Within the field of Natural Language Processing (NLP), the traditional approach for privacy was to apply anonymization techniques such as k-anonymity (Sweeney, 2002) and its variants. While this offers an intuitive way of expressing privacy guarantees as a function of an aggregation parameter k, all such methods are provably non-private (Korolova et al., 2009). Given the sheer increase in data gathering occurring across a multiplicity of connected platforms – a great number of which is being done via user generated voice conversations, text queries, or other language based metadata (e.g., user annotations), it is imperative to advance the development of DP techniques in NLP.

Vector embeddings are a popular approach for capturing the "meaning" of text and a form of unsupervised learning useful for downstream tasks. Word embeddings were popularized via embedding schemes such as WORD2VEC (Mikolov et al., 2013), GLOVE (Pennington et al., 2014), and FASTTEXT (Bojanowski et al., 2017). There is also a growing literature on creating embeddings for sentences, documents, and other textual entities, in addition to embeddings in other domains such as in computer vision (Goodfellow et al., 2016).

Recent works such as (Fernandes et al., 2019; Feyisetan et al., 2019, 2020; Xu et al., 2020) have attempted to directly adapt the methods of DP to word embeddings by borrowing ideas from the privacy methods used for map location data (Andrés et al., 2013). In the DP literature, one standard way of achieving privacy is by adding properly calibrated noise to the output of a function (Dwork et al., 2006). This is also the premise behind these previously proposed DP for text techniques, which are based on adding noise to the vector representation of words in a high dimensional embedding space and additional post-processing steps. The

Proceedings of the First Workshop on Trustworthy Natural Language Processing, pages 15–27
June 10, 2021. ©2021 Association for Computational Linguistics

privacy guarantees of applying such a method is quite straightforward. However, the main issue is that the magnitude of the DP privacy noise scales with dimensionality of the vector, which leads to a considerable degradation to the utility when these techniques are applied to vectors produced through popular embedding techniques. In this paper, we seek to overcome this curse of dimensionality arising through the differential privacy requirement. Also unlike previous results which were focused on word embeddings, we focus on the general problem of privately releasing vector embeddings, thus making our scheme more widely applicable.

1.1 Related Work

Vector representations of words, sentences, and documents, have all become basic building blocks in NLP pipelines and algorithms. Hence, it is natural to consider privacy mechanisms that target these representations. The most relevant to this paper is the privacy mechanism proposed in (Feyisetan et al., 2020) that works by computing the vector representation x of a word in the embedding space, applying noise N calibrated to the global metric sensitivity to obtain a perturbed vector $v = x + N$, and then swapping the original word another word whose embedding is closest to v. (Feyisetan et al., 2020) showed that this mechanism satisfies the $(\epsilon, 0)$-Lipschitz privacy definition. However, the issue with this mechanism is that the magnitude (norm) of the added noise is proportional to d, which we avoid by projecting these vectors down before the noise addition step. Our focus here is also more general and not just on word embeddings. Additionally, we provide theoretical guarantees on our privatized vectors. We experimentally compare with this approach.

The privacy mechanisms of (Fernandes et al., 2019; Feyisetan et al., 2019) are also based on similar noise addition ideas. However, (Fernandes et al., 2019) utilized the Earth mover metric to measure distances (instead of Euclidean), and (Feyisetan et al., 2019) perturb vector representations of words in high dimensional Hyperbolic space (instead of a real space). In this paper, we focus on the Euclidean space as it captures the most common choice of metric space with vector models.

Over the past decade, a large body of work has been developed to design basic algorithms and tools for achieving DP, understanding the privacy-utility trade-offs in different data access setups, and on integrating DP with machine learning and statistical inference. We refer the reader to (Dwork and Roth, 2013) for a more comprehensive overview.

Dimensionality reduction for word embeddings using PCA was explored in (Raunak et al., 2019) for computational efficiency purposes. In this paper, we use random projections for dimensionality reduction that helps with reducing the magnitude of noise needed for privacy. Another issue with PCA like scheme is that there are strong lower bounds (that scale with dimension of the vectors d) on the amount of distortion needed for achieving differentially private PCA in the local privacy model (Wang and Xu, 2020).

Random projections have been used as a tool to design differentially private algorithms in other problem settings too (Blocki et al., 2012; Wang et al., 2015; Kenthapadi et al., 2013; Zhou et al., 2009; Kasiviswanathan and Jin, 2016).

2 Preliminaries

We denote $[n] = \{1, \ldots, n\}$. Vectors are in column-wise fashion. We measure the distance between embeddings through the Euclidean metric. For a vector x, we set $\|x\|$ to denote the Euclidean (L_2-) norm and $\|x\|_1$ denotes its L_1-norm. For sets S, T, the Minkowski sum $S + T = \{a + b : a \in S, b \in T\}$. $\mathcal{N}(0, \sigma^2)$ denotes the Gaussian distribution with mean 0 and variance σ^2.

2.1 Privacy Motivations for Text

The privacy concerns around word embedding vectors stem from how they are created. For example, embeddings created using neural models inherit the side effects of unintended memorizations that come with such models (Carlini et al., 2019). Similarly it has been demonstrated that text generation models that encode language representations also suffer from various degrees of information leakage (Song and Shmatikov, 2019; Lyu et al., 2020). While this might not be concerning for off the shelf models trained on public data, it becomes important for word embeddings trained on non-public data.

Recent studies (Song and Raghunathan, 2020; Thomas et al., 2020) have shown that word embeddings are vulnerable to 3 types of attacks (1) *embedding inversion* where the vectors can be used to recreate some of the input training data; (2) *attribution inference* occurs when sensitive attributes (such as authorship) of the input data are revealed even when they are independent of the task at hand;

and (3) *membership inference* where an attacker is able to determine if data from a particular user was used to train the word embedding model.

The privacy consequences are further amplified depending on the domain of data under consideration. For example, a study by (Abdalla et al., 2020) on word embeddings in the medical domain demonstrated that: (1) they were able to reconstruct up to 68.5% of full names based on the embeddings i.e., *embedding inversion*; (2) they were able to retrieve associated sensitive information to specific patients in the corpus i.e., *attribution inference*; and (3) by using the distance between the vector of a patient's name and a billing code, they could differentiate between patients that were billed, and those that weren't i.e., *membership inference*.

These findings all underscore the need to release text embeddings using a rigorous notion of privacy, such as differential privacy, that preserves user privacy and mitigates the attacks described above.

2.2 Background on Differential Privacy.

Differential privacy (Dwork et al., 2006) gives a formal standard of privacy, requiring that, for all pairs of datasets that differ in one element, the distribution of outputs should be similar. In this paper, we use the notion of local differential privacy (LDP) (Kasiviswanathan et al., 2011).

A randomized algorithm $\mathcal{A} : \mathcal{X} \to \mathcal{Z}$ is (ϵ, δ)-local differentially private (LDP) if for any two data $x, x' \in \mathcal{X}$ and all (measurable) sets $U \subseteq \mathcal{Z}$,

$$\mathsf{Pr}[\mathcal{A}(x) \in U] \leq e^{\epsilon}\mathsf{Pr}[\mathcal{A}(x') \in U] + \delta.$$

The probability is taken over the random coins of $\mathcal{A}$. Here, we think of δ as being cryptographically small, whereas ϵ is typically thought of as a moderately small constant. The above definition considers every pair of x and x' (considered as adjacent for the purposes of DP). The LDP notion requires that the given x has a non-negligible probability of being transformed into any other $x' \in \mathcal{X}$ no matter how unrelated (far) x and x' are. However, for text embeddings, this strong requirement makes it virtually impossible to enforce that the semantics of a word are approximately preserved by the privatized vector (Feyisetan et al., 2020). To address this problem, we work with a modification of the above definition, referred to as Lipschitz (or metric) privacy, that is better suited for metric spaces defined through embedding models. Lipschitz privacy is closely related to LDP where the adjacency relation is defined through the Hamming metric, but also generalizes to include Euclidean, Manhattan, and Chebyshev metrics, among others (Chatzikokolakis et al., 2013; Andrés et al., 2013; Chatzikokolakis et al., 2015; Fernandes et al., 2019; Feyisetan et al., 2019, 2020). Similar to differential privacy, Lipschitz privacy is preserved under post-processing and composition of mechanisms (Koufogiannis et al., 2016).

Definition 1 (Lipschitz Privacy (Dwork et al., 2006; Chatzikokolakis et al., 2013))**.** *Let $(\mathcal{X}, d)$ be a metric space. A randomized algorithm $\mathcal{A} : \mathcal{X} \to \mathcal{Z}$ is (ϵ, δ)-Lipschitz private if for any two data $x, x' \in \mathcal{X}$ and all (measurable) sets $U \subseteq \mathcal{Z}$,*

$$\mathsf{Pr}[\mathcal{A}(x) \in U] \leq \exp(\epsilon d(x, x'))\mathsf{Pr}[\mathcal{A}(x') \in U] + \delta.$$

An alternate equivalent way of stating this would be to say that with probability at least $1 - \delta$, over a drawn from either $\mathcal{A}(x)$ or $\mathcal{A}(x')$, we have $|\ln \mathsf{Pr}[\mathcal{A}(x) = a] - \ln \mathsf{Pr}[\mathcal{A}(x') = a]| \leq \epsilon d(x, x')$.

The key difference between Lipschitz privacy and LDP is that the latter corresponds to a particular instance of the former when the distance function is given by $d(x, x') = 1$ for every $x \neq x'$.

In this paper, the metric space of interest is defined by embeddings which organize discrete objects in a continuous real space such that objects that are "similar" result in vectors are "close" in the embedded space. For the distance measure, we focus on the Euclidean metric, $d(x, x') = \|x - x'\|$ that is known to capture semantic similarity between discrete words in a continuous space.

For a function, $f : \mathcal{X} \to \mathbb{R}^m$, the most basic technique in differential privacy to release $f(x)$ is to answer $f(x) + \nu$, where ν is instance-independent additive noise (e.g., Laplace or Gaussian) with standard deviation proportional to the *global sensitivity* of the function f.

Definition 2 (Global sensitivity)**.** *For a function $f : \mathcal{X} \to \mathbb{R}^m$, define the global sensitivity of f as*

$$\Delta_f = \max_{x,x' \in \mathcal{X}} \frac{\|f(x) - f(x')\|}{\|x - x'\|}.$$

2.3 Dimensionality Reduction.

Dimensionality reduction is the problem of embedding a set from high-dimensions into a low-dimensional space, while preserving certain properties of the original high-dimensional set. Perhaps the most fundamental result for dimensionality reduction is the Johnson-Lindenstrauss (JL) lemma which states that any set of p points in high dimensions can be embedded into $O(\log(p)/\beta^2)$ dimensions, while preserving the Euclidean norm of all points within a multiplicative factor between $1 - \beta$ and $1 + \beta$. In fact, one could embed an infinite continuum of points into lower dimensions while preserving the Euclidean norm of all point up to a multiplicative distortion. A classical result due to (Gordon, 1988) characterizes the relation between the "size" of the set and the required dimensionality of the embedding on the unit sphere. Before stating the result, we need to introduce the notion of Gaussian width which captures the L_2-geometric complexity of $\mathcal{X}$.

Definition 3 (Gaussian Width). *Given a closed set $\mathcal{X} \subset \mathbb{R}^d$, its Gaussian width $\omega(\mathcal{X})$ is defined as:*

$$\omega(\mathcal{X}) = \mathbb{E}_{g \in \mathcal{N}(0,1)^d} [\sup_{x \in \mathcal{X}} \langle x, g \rangle].$$

Many popular sets have low Gaussian width (Vershynin, 2016). For example, if $\mathcal{X}$ contains vector in $\mathbb{R}^d$ that are c-sparse (at most c non-zero elements) then $\omega(\mathcal{X}) = \sqrt{c \log(d/c)}$. If $\mathcal{X}$ contains vectors that are sparse in the L_1-sense, say $\forall x \in \mathcal{X}$, $\|x\|_1 \leq c$, then $\omega(\mathcal{X}) = O(c\sqrt{\log d})$. Similarly if $\mathcal{X}$ is the d-dimensional probability simplex, then $\omega(\mathcal{X}) = O(\sqrt{\log d})$. Notice that in all these cases $\omega(\mathcal{X})^2$ is exponentially smaller than d.

The following is a restatement of the original Gordon's theorem that is better suited for this paper.

Theorem 1 (Gordon's Theorem (Gordon, 1988)). *Let $\beta \in (0,1)$, $\mathcal{X}$ be a subset of the unit d-dimensional sphere and let $\Phi \in \mathbb{R}^{m \times d}$ be a matrix with i.i.d. entries from $\mathcal{N}(0, 1/m)$. Then, $|\|\Phi x\| - 1| \leq \beta$, holds for all $x \in \mathcal{X}$ with probability at least $1 - 2\exp(-\gamma^2/2)$ if $m = \Omega((\omega(\mathcal{X}) + \gamma)^2/\beta^2)$.*

In particular, for a set of points $\mathcal{X} \subset \mathbb{R}^d$, we have the following:
$\Pr[\forall x \in \mathcal{X}, |\|\Phi x\| - \|x\|| \leq \beta\|x\|] \geq 1 - \gamma$, *if* $m = \Omega((\omega(\mathcal{X}) + \sqrt{\log(1/\gamma)})^2/\beta^2)$

Since for any set $\mathcal{X}$ with $|\mathcal{X}| = p$, $w(\mathcal{X})^2 \leq \log p$, therefore the above theorem is a generalization of the JL lemma. By a simple manipulation and adjusting β, Theorem 1 can be restated for preserving inner-products.

Corollary 2. *Under the setting of Theorem 1, for a set of points $\mathcal{X}$ in $\mathbb{R}^d$,*

$$|\langle \Phi x, \Phi x' \rangle - \langle x, x' \rangle| \leq \beta\|x\|\|x'\|,$$

holds for all $x, x' \in \mathcal{X}$ with probability at least $1 - \gamma$, if $m = \Omega((\omega(\mathcal{X}) + \sqrt{\log(1/\gamma)})^2/\beta^2)$.

The above result also holds if we replace the Gaussian random matrix Φ by a sparse random matrix (Bourgain et al., 2015). For simplicity, we use a Gaussian matrix Φ for projection.

3 Our Approach

The main issue arising in constructing differentially private vector embeddings is that a direct noise addition to the vectors (such as in (Feyisetan et al., 2020)) would require that the L_2-norm of the noise vector scales almost linearly with the dimensionality of the vector. To overcome this dimension dependence, our mechanism is based on the idea of performing a dimensionality reduction and then adding noise to the projected vector. By carefully balancing the dimensionality of the vectors with the magnitude of the noise needed for DP, the mechanism achieves a superior performance overall.

We will add noise calibrated to the sensitivity of the dimensionality reduction function. The noise is sampled from a d-dimensional distribution with density $p(z) \propto \exp(-\epsilon\|z\|/\Delta_f)$. Sampling from this distribution is simple as noted in (Wu et al., 2017).[1]. The following simple claim (that holds for all functions f) shows that this mechanism satisfies Definition 1. All the missing proofs from this section are collected in Appendix C.

Claim 3. *Let $f : \mathcal{X} \to \mathbb{R}^m$. Then publishing $\mathcal{A}(x) = f(x) + \kappa$ where κ is sampled from the distribution in $\mathbb{R}^m$ with density $p(z) \propto \exp(-\epsilon\|z\|/\Delta_f)$ satisfies $(\epsilon, 0)$-Lipschitz privacy.*

Let Φ be an $m \times d$ matrix with i.i.d. entries from $\mathcal{N}(0, 1/m)$. Consider an embedding model M. Let $\mathrm{Dom}(M)$ denote the domain and $\mathrm{Ran}(M) \subset \mathbb{R}^d$ denote the range of M. Define a function $f_\Phi : \mathrm{Ran}(M) \to \mathbb{R}^m$ as

$$f_\Phi(x) = \Phi x \text{ and } \Phi \in \mathbb{R}^{m \times d} \text{ i.i.d. from } \mathcal{N}(0, 1/m)\,. \quad (1)$$

Let us first investigate the global sensitivity of f_Φ using Theorem 1. Instead of considering a fixed bound on global sensitivity, we provide a probabilistic upper bound.

Lemma 4. *Let Φ be an $m \times d$ matrix with i.i.d. entries from $\mathcal{N}(0, 1/m)$. Let $\beta \in (0,1)$. If $m = \Omega((\omega(\mathrm{Ran}(M)) + \sqrt{\log(1/\delta)})^2/\beta^2)$, then with probability, at least $1 - \delta$, $\Delta_{f_\Phi} \leq 1 + \beta$.*

Let $\beta \in (0,1)$ be a fixed constant. Consider the mechanism which publishes $\mathcal{A}(x) = f_\Phi(x) + \kappa$ where κ is drawn from the distribution with density $p(z) \propto \exp(-\epsilon\|z\|/(1+\beta))$. Given a set of sensitive words $(x_1, \ldots, x_n)$, we can apply $\mathcal{A}(x_i)$ to each word x_i, to release $\mathcal{A}(x_1), \ldots, \mathcal{A}(x_n) \in \mathbb{R}^m$.

[1] The idea is to first sample a uniform vector in the unit sphere in $\mathbb{R}^m$, say v and to sample a magnitude l from the Gamma distribution $\Gamma(m, \Delta_f/\epsilon)$, and output $\kappa = lv$

Algorithm PrivEmb summarizes the mechanism. Since each vector is perturbed independently, the algorithm can be invoked locally. We now establish the privacy guarantee of PrivEmb. The δ factor comes in from Lemma 4 because we only have a probabilistic bound on the global sensitivity, i.e., there exists pairs of x, x' for whom the bound on global sensitivity of $1+\beta$ could fail.

For example, imagine a situation where there are n users each having a sensitive word (embedding). Given access to a common Φ, they can perturb their word locally and transmit only the perturbed vector.

Algorithm 1: PrivEmb

Input: $x_1, \ldots, x_n \in \mathrm{Ran}(M)$ for model M, privacy parameters $\epsilon, \delta > 0$, and dimensionality reduction parameter $\beta \in (0,1)$
Output: private vector embeddings $w_1, \ldots, w_n$
Let $m = \Omega((\omega(\mathrm{Ran}(M)) + \sqrt{\log(1/\delta)})^2/\beta^2)$
Let $\Phi \sim_{i.i.d.} \mathcal{N}(0, 1/m)$
for $i \in \{1, \ldots, n\}$ **do**
  $w_i = \Phi x_i + \kappa_i$ where κ_i is i.i.d. from the distr. with density $p(z) \propto \exp(-\epsilon\|z\|/(1+\beta))$
release $(w_1, \ldots, w_n)$

Using Claim 3 and Lemma 4, we now establish that privacy proof for Algorithm PrivEmb.

Proposition 5. *Algorithm* PrivEmb *is* (ϵ, δ)*-Lipschitz private. Let* $\beta \in (0,1)$*,* $\delta > 0$*,* $\epsilon > 0$*, and* $m = \Omega((\omega(\mathrm{Ran}(M)) + \sqrt{\log(1/\delta)})^2/\beta^2)$*. Let* Φ *be an* $m \times d$ *matrix with i.i.d. entries from* $\mathcal{N}(0, 1/m)$*. Then publishing* $\mathcal{A}(x) = f_\Phi(x) + \kappa$ *where* κ *is drawn from the distribution in* $\mathbb{R}^m$ *with density* $p(z) \propto \exp(-\epsilon\|z\|/(1+\beta))$ *is* (ϵ, δ)*-Lipschitz private.*

It is important to note that the β does not affect the privacy analysis, i.e., for any input parameter β, Algorithm PrivEmb is (ϵ, δ)-Lipschitz private.

While the idea behind Algorithm PrivEmb is simple, it is widely applicable and effective. As an example consider vector representation of text such as through Bag-of-K-grams, which creates representations that are sparse in some very high-dimensional space (say c-sparse vectors). In this case, even though d could be extremely large, we can project these vectors to $\approx c\log(d/c)$-dimensional space (due to their low Gaussian width) and add noise in the projected space for achieving privacy. On the other hand, the privacy mechanism of (Feyisetan et al., 2020), with noise magnitude proportional to d will completely destroy the information in these vectors.

4 Utility Analysis of Alg. PrivEmb

We now provide utility performance bounds for Algorithm PrivEmb. As mentioned earlier these are the first theoretical analysis for any private vector embedding scheme. We start with two important properties of interest based on distances and inner-products that commonly arise when dealing with text embeddings. Our next result compares the loss of a linear model trained on these private vector embeddings to loss of a similar model trained on the original vector embeddings. All our error bounds depend on $m \approx \omega(\mathrm{Ran}(M))^2$.

We start with a simple observation about the magnitude of the noise vector. Consider κ drawn from the noise distribution with density $p(z) \propto \exp(-\epsilon\|z\|/(1+\beta))$. The Euclidean norm of κ is distributed according to the Gamma distribution $\Gamma(m, (1+\beta)/\epsilon)$ (Wu et al., 2017) and satisfies the following bound.

Claim 6 ((Wu et al., 2017; Chaudhuri et al., 2011))**.** *For the noise vector* κ*, we have that with probability at least* $1-\gamma$*,* $\|\kappa\| \leq (m\ln(m/\gamma)(1+\beta))/\epsilon$*.*

Since $\beta < 1$, we can simplify the right hand side of the above claim to $(2m\ln(m/\gamma))/\epsilon$. Let τ be the maximum Euclidean norm of the vectors $x_1, \ldots, x_n$, i.e., $\forall i \in [n]$, $\|x_i\| \leq \tau$.

4.1 Distance Approximation Guarantee

Our first result compares the distances between the private vectors and between the original vectors.

Proposition 7. *Consider Algorithm* PrivEmb*. With probability at least* $1-\delta$*, for all pairs* $x_i, x_j \in (x_1, \ldots, x_n)$*,* $|\|w_i - w_j\| - \|x_i - x_j\|| \leq 2\beta\tau + 4(m\ln(2nm/\delta))/\epsilon$*.*

As a baseline consider the privatization mechanism proposed by (Feyisetan et al., 2020) which computes a privatized version of an embedding vector x by adding noise N to the original vector x. Formally, (Feyisetan et al., 2020) defined a mechanism where the private vector v_i is constructed from x_i as follows: $v_i = x_i + N_i$ where N_i is drawn from the distribution in $\mathbb{R}^d$ with density $p(z) \propto \exp(-\epsilon\|z\|)$ to x. Since the noise vector N_i is now d-dimensional, its Euclidean norm will tightly concentrate around its mean $\mathbb{E}[\|N_i\|] = O(d)$. Therefore, with high probability, $|\|v_i - v_j\| - \|x_i - x_j\|| = \Omega(d)$ holds for the mechanism proposed in (Feyisetan et al., 2020). However, in our mechanism, the dependence on d is replaced by m which as argued above is generally much smaller than d. On the flip side though, PRIVEMB satisfies (ϵ, δ)-Lipschitz privacy for $\delta > 0$, whereas the mechanism in (Feyisetan et al., 2020) achieves the stronger $(\epsilon, 0)$-Lipschitz privacy.

4.2 Inner-Product Approximation Guarantee

Word embeddings seek to capture word similarity, so similar words (e.g., synonyms) have embeddings with high inner product. We now compare the inner product between the private vectors to the inner product between the original embedding vectors.

Proposition 8. *Consider Algorithm* PRIVEMB. *With probability at least* $1 - \delta$, *for all pairs* $x_i, x_j \in (x_1, \ldots, x_n)$, $|\langle w_i, w_j \rangle - \langle x_i, x_j \rangle| \leq \beta\tau^2 + 8\tau m \ln(2nm/\delta)/\epsilon + (2m\ln(2nm/\delta))^2/\epsilon^2$.

4.3 Performance on Linear Models

We now discuss about the performance of the private vectors $(w_1, \ldots, w_n)$ when used with common machine learning models. Given n datapoints, $(x_1, y_1), \ldots, (x_n, y_n)$ drawn from some universe $\mathbb{R}^d \times \mathbb{R}$ (where y_i represents the label on point x_i), we consider the problem of learning a linear model on this labeled data. We assume that x_i's are sensitive whereas the y_i's are publicly known. Such situations arise commonly in practice. For example, consider a drug company investigating the effectiveness of a drug trail over n users. Here, y_i could represent the response to the drug for user i which is known to the drug company, whereas x_i could encode the medical history of user i which the user would like to keep private.

We focus on a broad class of models, where the loss functions have the form, $\ell(\langle x, \theta \rangle; y)$ for parameter $\theta \in \mathbb{R}^d$, where $\ell : \mathbb{R} \times \mathbb{R} \to \mathbb{R}$. This captures a variety of learning problems, e.g., the linear regression is captured by setting $\ell(\langle x, \theta \rangle; y) = (y - \langle x, \theta \rangle)^2$, logistic regression is captured by setting $\ell(\langle x, \theta \rangle; y) = \ln(1 + \exp(-y\langle x, \theta \rangle))$, support vector machine is captured by setting $\ell(\langle x, \theta \rangle; y) = \mathrm{hinge}(y\langle x, \theta \rangle)$, where $\mathrm{hinge}(a) = 1 - a$ if $a \leq 1$ and 0 otherwise. We assume that the function ℓ is convex and Lipschitz in the first parameter. Let λ_ℓ denote the Lipschitz parameter of the loss function ℓ over the first parameter, i.e., $|\ell(a; y) - \ell(b; y)| \leq \lambda_\ell |a - b|$ for all $a, b \in \mathbb{R}$.

On the data $(x_1, y_1), \ldots, (x_n, y_n)$, the (empirical) training loss for a parameter θ is defined as: $\frac{1}{n}\sum_{i=1}^n \ell(\langle x_i, \theta \rangle; y_i)$ and the goal in training (empirical risk minimization) is to minimize this loss over a parameter space Θ. Let $\theta^\star$ be a true minimizer of $\frac{1}{n}\sum_{i=1}^n \ell(\langle x_i, \theta \rangle; y_i)$, i.e., $\theta^\star \in \mathrm{argmin}_{\theta \in \Theta} \frac{1}{n}\sum_{i=1}^n \ell(\langle x_i, \theta \rangle; y_i)$.

Our goal will be to compare the loss of the model trained on the privatized points $(w_1, y_1), \ldots (w_n, y_n)$ where the w_i's are produced by Algorithm PRIVEMB to the true minimum loss $(= \frac{1}{n}\sum_{i=1}^n \ell(\langle x_i, \theta^\star \rangle; y_i))$. Let $\|\Theta\|$ defined as $\sup_{\theta \in \Theta} \|\theta\|$ denote the diameter of Θ. The following proposition states our result.

Proposition 9. *Consider Algorithm* PRIVEMB. *With probability at least* $1 - \delta$,

$$\min_{\theta \in \Theta} \frac{1}{n} \sum_{i=1}^{n} \ell(\langle w_i, \Phi\theta \rangle; y_i) \leq \frac{1}{n} \sum_{i=1}^{n} \ell(\langle x_i, \theta^\star \rangle; y_i) + \frac{4\lambda_\ell (m \ln(2nm/\delta))\|\Theta\|}{\epsilon} + \lambda_\ell \beta\tau\|\Theta\|.$$

In the above result the error terms will be negligible if $\beta \ll 1/(\lambda_\ell \tau\|\Theta\|)$ and $\epsilon \gg \lambda_\ell(m\ln(2nm/\delta))\|\Theta\|$. Though in our experiments (see Section 5), we notice good performance with private vectors even when β and ϵ don't satisfy these conditions.

Another point to note is that our setting, where we train ML models over a differentially private data release, is different from traditional literature on differentially private empirical risk minimization where the goal is to release only a private version of model parameter θ, and not the data itself, see e.g., (Chaudhuri et al., 2011; Bassily et al., 2014). In particular, this means that the results from traditional differentially private empirical risk minimization do not carry over to our setting. Our data release setup allows training any number of ML models on the private vectors without having to pay for the cost of composition on the privacy guarantees (as post-processing does not affect the privacy guarantee), which is a desirable property.

5 Experimental Evaluations

We carry out four experiments to demonstrate the improvement of our approach (Algorithm PRIVEMB), denoted as **M2**, over $(\epsilon, 0)$-Lipschitz privacy mechanism proposed in (Feyisetan et al., 2020) (denoted by **M1**).[2] The first three map to the theoretical guarantees described Section 4, i.e., (1) distance approximation guarantee, (2) inner-product approximation guarantee, and (3) performance on linear models. The final experiment provides further evidence for performance of

[2]We choose this mechanism as the baseline as in this setup it achieves the current state-of-the-art utililty guarantees.

using these private vectors for downstream classification tasks. All our experiments are on embeddings generated by GLOVE (Pennington et al., 2014) and FASTTEXT (Bojanowski et al., 2017). The dimensionality of the embedding $d = 300$ in both cases. Due to space constraints, we present the FASTTEXT results in Appendix B.

The value of δ is kept constant for all experiments (involving our scheme) at $1e-6$. We set $\omega(\mathrm{Ran}(M)) = \sqrt{\log d}$. The parameter β only affects the utility guarantee, and Algorithm PRIVEMB is always (ϵ, δ)-Lipschitz private for any value of β. In our experiments, corroborating our theoretical guarantees, we do vary β to illustrate the effect of β on the guarantees. Remember that higher values of β results in lower-dimensional vectors, so setting β appropriately lets one trade-off between the loss of utility due to dimension reduction vs. the gain in the utility due to lesser noise needed for lower-dimensional vectors.

We also vary the privacy parameter ϵ in our experiments. While lower values ϵ are certainly desirable, it is widely known that differentially private algorithms for certain problems (such as those arising in complex domains such as NLP) require slightly larger ϵ values to provide reasonable utility in practice (Fernandes et al., 2019; Feyisetan et al., 2020; Xie et al., 2018; Ma et al., 2020). For example, the related work on differential privately releasing text embeddings from Fernandes *et al.* (Fernandes et al., 2019) and Feyisetan *et al.* (Feyisetan et al., 2020) report values of ϵ of up to 20 and 30 depending on the dimensionality of the space.

5.1 Distance Approximation Guarantees

This experiment compares the distance between pairs of private vectors to that between the corresponding original vectors. We sampled 100 word vectors from the vocabulary. For each of these 100 vectors, we compare the distance to another set of 100 randomly sampled vectors. These 100×100 pair of vectors were kept constant across all experiment runs. For each embedding model, we compared $|\|v_i - v_j\| - \|x_i - x_j\||$ where the v_i's are generated by the schemed in (Feyisetan et al., 2020) (**M1**), to $|\|w_i - w_j\| - \|x_i - x_j\||$ where the w_i's are generated by our scheme (**M2**). The experiments were carried out at values of $\epsilon = 1, 2,$ and 5 for **M1** and **M2**, while varying the values of β for **M2** between 0.5 and 0.7.

Results. The results in Fig. 1 show the experiment

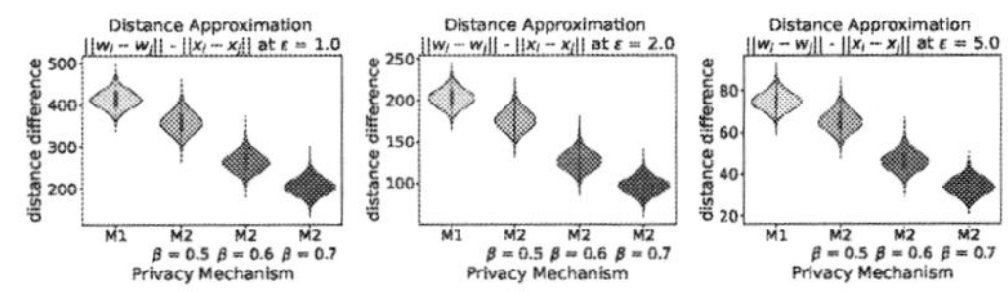

Figure 1: Distance Approximation (GLOVE)

outcomes across the different values of ϵ, β, and embeddings. Lower values on the $y-$axis indicate better results in that the distance between the private vectors are a good approximation to the actual distances between the original vectors. Overall, the guarantees of our approach **M2** are better than **M1** as observed by the smaller distance differences across all conditions. Next, the results also highlight that for both mechanisms, as expected, the guarantees get better as ϵ increases, due to the introduction of less noise (note the different scales across ϵ). Finally, the results reveal that for a given value of ϵ, as the value of β increases, the guarantees of our scheme improve. This can be viewed through the guarantees of Proposition 7, which consists of two terms, the first term increases with β and the second term due to its dependence on $1/\beta^2$ (through m) decreases with β. Since the second (noise) term generally dominates, we get an improvement with β, suggesting that it is advantageous to pick a larger β in practice.

5.2 Inner Prod Approximation Guarantees

This experiment compares the inner product between pairs of private vectors to that between the corresponding original vectors. The setup here is identical to the distance approximation experiments (i.e., the same 100×100 word pairs and mix of ϵ and β). The results capture $|\langle w_i, w_j \rangle - \langle x_i, x_j \rangle|$.

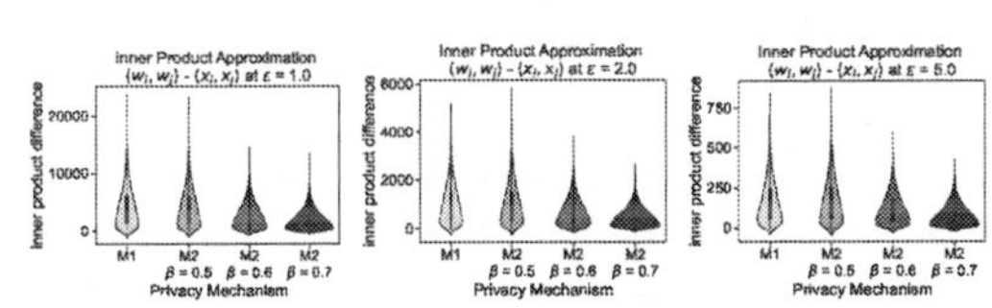

Figure 2: Inner Prod Approximation (GLOVE)

Results. The results in Fig. 2 show the experiment outcomes across ϵ, β, and embeddings. Similar to the findings in Fig. 1, the results of **M2** are an improvement over **M1** with the same patterns of improvement. For a fixed privacy budget, the performance of **M2** is better than that of **M1** and the gap increases as β increases. Again this suggests that one should pick a larger β.

	Non-Private Baselines		M1: $\epsilon = 10$		M2: $\epsilon = 10, \beta = 0.9$	
Dataset	InferSent	SkipThought	TRAIN ACC	TEST ACC	TRAIN ACC	TEST ACC
MR (Pang and Lee, 2005)	81.10	79.40	58.10	55.61	57.76	58.11
CR (Hu and Liu, 2004)	86.30	83.10	68.32	63.97	72.52	71.02
MPQA (Wiebe et al., 2005)	90.20	89.30	78.76	77.98	77.84	78.86
SST-5 (Socher et al., 2013)	46.30	44.80	31.24	31.90	32.70	32.49
TREC-6 (Li and Roth, 2002)	88.20	88.40	60.54	53.20	62.53	73.00

Table 1: Training and test accuracy scores on classification tasks.

5.3 Performance on Linear Models

We built a simple binary SVM linear mode to classify single keywords into 2 classes: positive and negative based on their conveyed sentiment. The dataset used was a list from (Hu and Liu, 2004) consisting of 4783 negative and 2006 positive words. We selected a subset of words that occurred in both GLOVE and FASTTEXT embeddings and capped both lists to have an equal number of words. The resulting datasets each had 1899 words. The purpose of this experiment was to explore the behaviors of **M1** and **M2** at different values of ϵ and β for a linear model. Results shown are over 10 runs.

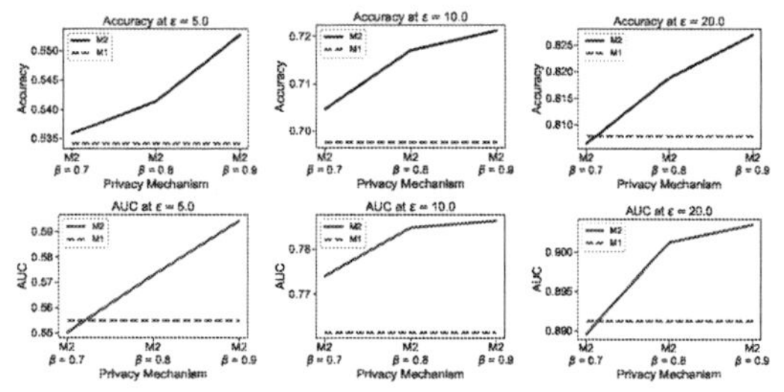

Figure 3: Linear Model Performance (GLOVE)

Results. The results on the performance on linear models are presented in Fig. 3. The performance metrics are (i) accuracy on a randomly selected 20% test set, and (ii) the area under the ROC curve (AUC). Higher values on the $y-$axis indicate better results. The findings follow from our first 2 experiments which demonstrate that for a fixed privacy ϵ guarantee, the utility of **M2** is better than that of **M1** and the gap between the performance of **M2** and **M1** increases as β increases.

5.4 Performance on NLP Datasets

We further evaluated **M2** against **M1** at a fixed value of ϵ and β on classification tasks on 5 NLP datasets. The experiments were done and can be replicated using SentEval (Conneau and Kiela, 2018), an evaluation toolkit for sentence embeddings by replacing the default embeddings with the private embeddings. From the previous experiments, we know that it is better to pick a larger β, so we set $\beta = 0.9$ here.

Results. Table 1 presents the results and summarizes the datasets: MR (Pang and Lee, 2005), CR (Hu and Liu, 2004), MPQA (Wiebe et al., 2005), SST-5 (Socher et al., 2013), and TREC-6 (Li and Roth, 2002). Table 1 presents the results from the experiments. We also present results of 2 non-private baselines on all the datasets based on Infersent and SkipThought described in (Conneau et al., 2017). The evaluation metrics were train and test accuracies, therefore, higher scores indicate better utility. Not surprisingly, because of the noise addition there is is a performance drop when we compare the private mechanisms to the non-private baselines. However, the results reinforce our findings that the utility afforded by **M2** are better than **M1** at fixed values of ϵ. Some of the improvements are remarkably significant e.g., $+7\%$ on the CR dataset, and $+20\%$ on TREC-6.

Summary of the Results. Overall, these experiments demonstrate that PRIVEMB offers better utility than the embedding privatization scheme of (Feyisetan et al., 2020).

6 Concluding Remarks

In this paper, we introduced an (ϵ, δ)-Lipschitz private algorithm for generating real valued embedding vectors. Our mechanism works by first reducing the dimensionality of the vectors though a random projection, then adding noise calibrated to the sensitivity of the dimensionality reduction function. The mechanism can be utilized for any well-defined embedding model including but not limited to word, sentence, and document embeddings. We prove theoretical bounds that show how various properties of interest important for vector embeddings are well-approximated through the private vectors, and our empirical results across multiple embedding models and NLP datasets demonstrate the superior utility guarantees.

References

Mohamed Abdalla, Moustafa Abdalla, Graeme Hirst, and Frank Rudzicz. 2020. Exploring the privacy-preserving properties of word embeddings: Algorithmic validation study. *Journal of medical Internet research*, 22(7):e18055.

Miguel E Andrés, Nicolás E Bordenabe, Konstantinos Chatzikokolakis, and Catuscia Palamidessi. 2013. Geo-indistinguishability: Differential privacy for location-based systems. In *ACM CCS*, pages 901–914. ACM.

Raef Bassily, Adam Smith, and Abhradeep Thakurta. 2014. Differentially private empirical risk minimization: Efficient algorithms and tight error bounds. In *FOCS*. IEEE.

Jeremiah Blocki, Avrim Blum, Anupam Datta, and Or Sheffet. 2012. The johnson-lindenstrauss transform itself preserves differential privacy. In *2012 IEEE 53rd Annual Symposium on Foundations of Computer Science*, pages 410–419. IEEE.

Piotr Bojanowski, Edouard Grave, Armand Joulin, and Tomas Mikolov. 2017. Enriching word vectors with subword information. *TACL*, 5.

Jean Bourgain, Dirksen Sjoerd, and Jelani Nelson. 2015. Toward a unified theory of sparse dimensionality reduction in euclidean space. In *Proceedings of the 47th ACM Symposium on Theory of Computing*. Association for Computing Machinery.

Nicholas Carlini, Chang Liu, Úlfar Erlingsson, Jernej Kos, and Dawn Song. 2019. The secret sharer: Evaluating and testing unintended memorization in neural networks. In *28th {USENIX} Security Symposium ({USENIX} Security 19)*, pages 267–284.

Konstantinos Chatzikokolakis, Miguel E Andrés, Nicolás Emilio Bordenabe, and Catuscia Palamidessi. 2013. Broadening the scope of differential privacy using metrics. In *PETS*.

Konstantinos Chatzikokolakis, Catuscia Palamidessi, and Marco Stronati. 2015. Constructing elastic distinguishability metrics for location privacy. *PETS*.

Kamalika Chaudhuri, Claire Monteleoni, and Anand D Sarwate. 2011. Differentially private empirical risk minimization. *Journal of Machine Learning Research*, 12(3).

Alexis Conneau and Douwe Kiela. 2018. Senteval: An evaluation toolkit for universal sentence representations. *arXiv preprint arXiv:1803.05449*.

Alexis Conneau, Douwe Kiela, Holger Schwenk, Loïc Barrault, and Antoine Bordes. 2017. Supervised learning of universal sentence representations from natural language inference data. In *EMNLP*.

Aref Dajani, Amy Lauger, Phyllis Singer, Daniel Kifer, Jerome Reiter, Ashwin Machanavajjhala, Simon Garfinkel, Scot Dahl, Matthew Graham, Vishesh Karwa, Hang Kim, Philip Leclerc, Ian Schmutte, William Sexton, Lars Vilhuber, and John Abowd. 2017. The modernization of statistical disclosure limitation at the u.s. census bureau. *Census Scientific Advisory Commitee Meetings*.

Cynthia Dwork, Frank McSherry, Kobbi Nissim, and Adam Smith. 2006. Calibrating noise to sensitivity in private data analysis. In *TCC*, pages 265–284. Springer.

Cynthia Dwork and Aaron Roth. 2013. The algorithmic foundations of differential privacy. *Theoretical Computer Science*, 9(3-4).

Úlfar Erlingsson, Vasyl Pihur, and Aleksandra Korolova. 2014. Rappor: Randomized aggregatable privacy-preserving ordinal response. In *ACM SIGSAC CCS*.

Natasha Fernandes, Mark Dras, and Annabelle McIver. 2019. Generalised differential privacy for text document processing. *Principles of Security and Trust*.

Oluwaseyi Feyisetan, Borja Balle, Thomas Drake, and Tom Diethe. 2020. Privacy- and utility-preserving textual analysis via calibrated multivariate perturbations. In *ACM WSDM*.

Oluwaseyi Feyisetan, Tom Diethe, and Thomas Drake. 2019. Leveraging hierarchical representations for preserving privacy and utility in text. In *IEEE ICDM*.

Ian Goodfellow, Yoshua Bengio, and Aaron Courville. 2016. *Deep learning*. MIT press.

Yehoram Gordon. 1988. *On Milman's inequality and random subspaces which escape through a mesh in* $\mathbb{R}^n$. Springer.

Minqing Hu and Bing Liu. 2004. Mining and summarizing customer reviews. In *ACM SIGKDD*, pages 168–177.

Shiva Kasiviswanathan, Homin Lee, Kobbi Nissim, Sofya Raskhodnikova, and Adam Smith. 2011. What can we learn privately? *SIAM Journal on Computing*, 40(3).

Shiva Prasad Kasiviswanathan and Hongxia Jin. 2016. Efficient private empirical risk minimization for high-dimensional learning. In *International Conference on Machine Learning*, pages 488–497.

Krishnaram Kenthapadi, Aleksandra Korolova, Ilya Mironov, and Nina Mishra. 2013. Privacy via the johnson-lindenstrauss transform. *Journal of Privacy and Confidentiality*, 5(1):39–71.

Aleksandra Korolova, Krishnaram Kenthapadi, Nina Mishra, and Alexandros Ntoulas. 2009. Releasing search queries and clicks privately. In *WebConf*. ACM.

Fragkiskos Koufogiannis, Shuo Han, and George J Pappas. 2016. Gradual release of sensitive data under differential privacy. *Journal of Privacy and Confidentiality*, 7(2).

Xin Li and Dan Roth. 2002. Learning question classifiers. In *COLING*.

Lingjuan Lyu, Yitong Li, Xuanli He, and Tong Xiao. 2020. Towards differentially private text representations. In *Proceedings of the 43rd International ACM SIGIR Conference on Research and Development in Information Retrieval*, pages 1813–1816.

Chuan Ma, Jun Li, Ming Ding, Bo Liu, Kang Wei, Jian Weng, and H. Vincent Poor. 2020. Rdp-gan: A rényi-differential privacy based generative adversarial network.

Tomas Mikolov, Ilya Sutskever, Kai Chen, Greg S Corrado, and Jeff Dean. 2013. Distributed representations of words and phrases and their compositionality. In *NeurIPS*, pages 3111–3119.

Bo Pang and Lillian Lee. 2005. Seeing stars: Exploiting class relationships for sentiment categorization with respect to rating scales. In *ACL*.

Jeffrey Pennington, Richard Socher, and Christopher Manning. 2014. Glove: Global vectors for word representation. In *EMNLP*, pages 1532–1543.

Vikas Raunak, Vivek Gupta, and Florian Metze. 2019. Effective dimensionality reduction for word embeddings. In *Proceedings of the 4th Workshop on Representation Learning for NLP (RepL4NLP-2019)*, pages 235–243.

Richard Socher, Alex Perelygin, Jean Wu, Jason Chuang, Christopher D Manning, Andrew Ng, and Christopher Potts. 2013. Recursive deep models for semantic compositionality over a sentiment treebank. In *EMNLP*, pages 1631–1642.

Congzheng Song and Ananth Raghunathan. 2020. Information leakage in embedding models. *arXiv preprint arXiv:2004.00053*.

Congzheng Song and Vitaly Shmatikov. 2019. Auditing data provenance in text-generation models. In *ACM SIGKDD*.

Latanya Sweeney. 2002. k-anonymity: A model for protecting privacy. *IJUFKS*, 10(05):557–570.

Apple's Differential Privacy Team. 2017. Learning with privacy at scale. *Apple Machine Learning Journal*, 1(9).

Aleena Thomas, David Ifeoluwa Adelani, Ali Davody, Aditya Mogadala, and Dietrich Klakow. 2020. Investigating the impact of pre-trained word embeddings on memorization in neural networks. In *International Conference on Text, Speech, and Dialogue*, pages 273–281. Springer.

Uber Security. 2017. Uber releases open source project for differential privacy. `https://medium.com/uber-security-privacy/7892c82c42b6`.

Roman Vershynin. 2016. High dimensional probability. *An Introduction with Applications*.

Di Wang and Jinhui Xu. 2020. Principal component analysis in the local differential privacy model. *Theoretical Computer Science*, 809:296–312.

Yining Wang, Yu-Xiang Wang, and Aarti Singh. 2015. A deterministic analysis of noisy sparse subspace clustering for dimensionality-reduced data. In *Proceedings of the 32nd International Conference on Machine Learning (ICML-15)*, pages 1422–1431.

Janyce Wiebe, Theresa Wilson, and Claire Cardie. 2005. Annotating expressions of opinions and emotions in language. *LREC*.

Xi Wu, Fengan Li, Arun Kumar, Kamalika Chaudhuri, Somesh Jha, and Jeffrey Naughton. 2017. Bolt-on differential privacy for scalable stochastic gradient descent-based analytics. In *Proceedings of the 2017 ACM SIGMOD*, pages 1307–1322.

Liyang Xie, Kaixiang Lin, Shu Wang, Fei Wang, and Jiayu Zhou. 2018. Differentially private generative adversarial network.

Zekun Xu, Abhinav Aggarwal, Oluwaseyi Feyisetan, and Nathanael Teissier. 2020. A differentially private text perturbation method using regularized mahalanobis metric. In *Proceedings of the Second Workshop on Privacy in NLP at EMNLP 2020*, pages 7–17.

Shuheng Zhou, Katrina Ligett, and Larry Wasserman. 2009. Differential privacy with compression. In *Information Theory, 2009. ISIT 2009. IEEE International Symposium on*, pages 2718–2722. IEEE.

Supplementary Material for "Private Release of Text Embedding Vectors"

A Additional Experiments

We now investigate a slightly different setup where we perform the dimensionality reduction while training the embeddings (denoted as **A1**). So here instead of only assuming access to private embeddings vectors as in **M1** and **M2**, we also assume access to the corpus and training platform. Fig. 4 presents results (with linear models as in Experiment 3) on $50d$, $100d$, and $200d$ GLOVE embeddings, and corresponding setting of $\beta = 0.93, 0.66$ and 0.468 in **M2** to match the dimensionality. Unsurprisingly the results below show that **A1** obtains better results than **M2** where the dimensionality reduction happens post training. Mechanism **A1** however has two drawbacks compared to **M2**: (1) it assumes access to the original training corpus and platform which is not always accessible, and (2) it is more computationally expensive as it requires retraining the embeddings from scratch.

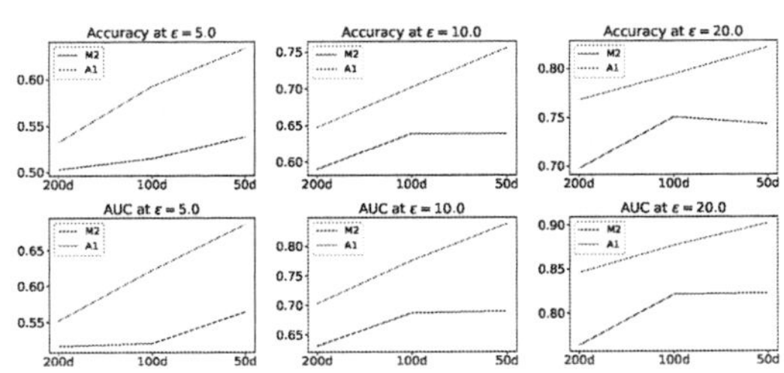

Figure 4: Comparing effects of dimensionality reduction during training vs. after (GLOVE).

B Missing Experiment Results on Fasttext

Experiment 1: Distance Approximation Guarantees.

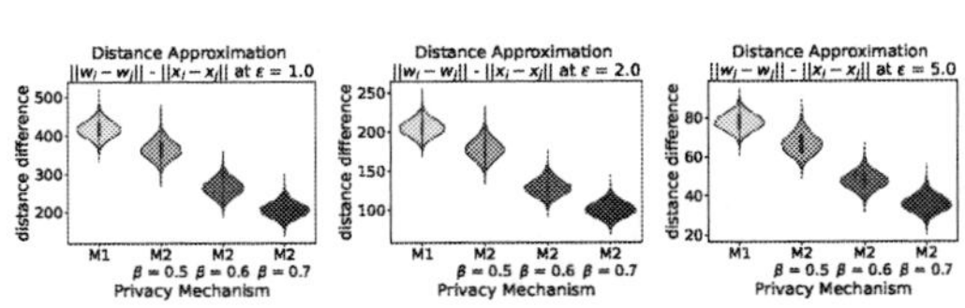

Figure 5: Distance Approximation Experiments (FASTTEXT)

Experiment 2: Inner Prod Approximation Guarantees.

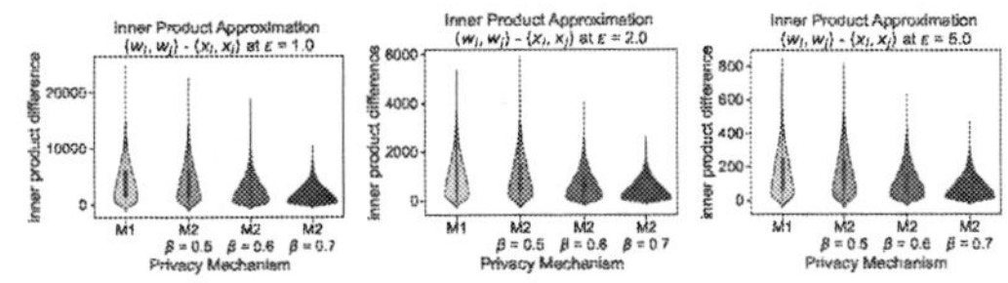

Figure 6: Inner Prod Approximation Experiment (FASTTEXT)

Experiment 3: Performance on Linear Models.

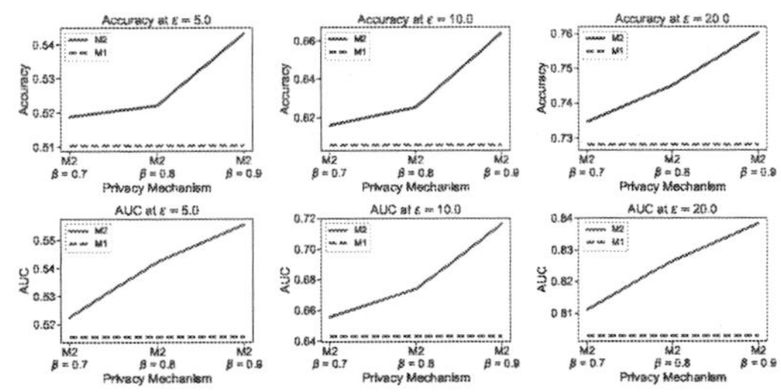

Figure 7: Linear Model Performance Experiments (FASTTEXT)

C Missing Details from Section 3

Claim 10 (Claim 3 Restated). *Let $f : \mathcal{X} \to \mathbb{R}^m$. Then publishing $\mathcal{A}(x) = f(x) + \kappa$ where κ is sampled from the distribution in $\mathbb{R}^m$ with density $p(z) \propto \exp(-\epsilon\|z\|/\Delta_f)$ satisfies $(\epsilon, 0)$-Lipschitz privacy.*

Proof. First note that $f(x) + \kappa$ has the same distribution as that of κ but with a different mean. Consider any $x, x' \in \mathcal{X}$. We will be interested in bounding the ratio $\Pr[\mathcal{A}(x) = w]/\Pr[\mathcal{A}(x') = w]$.

$$\frac{\Pr[\mathcal{A}(x) = w]}{\Pr[\mathcal{A}(x') = w]} = \frac{\exp(-\epsilon\|w - f(x)\|/\Delta_f)}{\exp(-\epsilon\|w - f(x')\|/\Delta_f)}$$
$$= \exp(\epsilon(\|w - f(x')\| - \|w - f(x)\|)/\Delta_f)$$
$$\leq \exp(\epsilon\|f(x) - f(x')\|/\Delta_f)$$
$$\leq \exp(\epsilon\|x - x'\|),$$

where the first inequality follows from triangle inequality and the last one follows from the definition of global sensitivity (Definition 2). Therefore, for any measurable set $U \subseteq \mathbb{R}^m$, $\Pr[\mathcal{A}(x) \in U] \leq \exp(\epsilon\|x - x'\|)\Pr[\mathcal{A}(x') \in U]$. □

Lemma 11 (Lemma 4 Restated). *Let Φ be an $m \times d$ matrix with i.i.d. entries from $\mathcal{N}(0, 1/m)$. Let $\beta \in (0, 1)$. If $m = \Omega((\omega(\mathrm{Ran}(M)) + \sqrt{\log(1/\delta)})^2/\beta^2)$, then with probability, at least $1 - \delta$, $\Delta_{f_\Phi} \leq 1 + \beta$.*

Proof. Consider the set $\mathrm{Ran}(M) - \mathrm{Ran}(M)$ (where $-$ denotes the Minkowski difference between the sets). By properties of the Gaussian width (see Section 2), the Gaussian width of this new set is at most $\omega(\mathrm{Ran}(M)) + \omega(\mathrm{Ran}(M)) \leq 2\omega(\mathrm{Ran}(M))$. From Theorem 1, under the above setting of m, with probability at least $1-\delta$,

$$\Delta_{f_\Phi} = \max_{x,x' \in \mathrm{Ran}(M)} \frac{\|\Phi x - \Phi x'\|}{\|x - x'\|} \leq (1+\beta).$$

This completes the proof. □

Proposition 12 (Proposition 5 Restated)**.** *Algorithm* PRIVEMB *is (ϵ, δ)-Lipschitz private.*

Proof. Let $\mathcal{A}(x) = f_\Phi(x) + \kappa = \Phi x + \kappa$ where κ is drawn from the distribution in $\mathbb{R}^m$ with density $p(z) \propto \exp(-\epsilon\|z\|/(1+\beta))$. Let $\mathcal{E}$ denote the event that the $\Delta_{f_\Phi} \leq 1 - \beta$. From Lemma 11, we know that over the choice of Φ, $\mathsf{Pr}[\mathcal{E}] \geq 1 - \delta$. Consider any $x, x' \in \mathrm{Ran}(M)$.

$$\begin{aligned}&\mathsf{Pr}[\mathcal{A}(x) = w] \\ &= \mathsf{Pr}[\mathcal{A}(x) = w \,|\, \mathcal{E}]\mathsf{Pr}[\mathcal{E}] + \mathsf{Pr}[\mathcal{A}(x) = w \,|\, \bar{\mathcal{E}}]\mathsf{Pr}[\bar{\mathcal{E}}] \\ &\leq \mathsf{Pr}[\mathcal{A}(x) = w \,|\, \mathcal{E}] + \delta,\end{aligned}$$

where we used that $\mathsf{Pr}[\mathcal{E}] \leq 1$, $\mathsf{Pr}[\mathcal{A}(x) = w \,|\, \bar{\mathcal{E}}] \leq 1$, and $\mathsf{Pr}[\bar{\mathcal{E}}] \leq \delta$. Now under $\mathcal{E}$, from Claim 10, $\mathsf{Pr}[\mathcal{A}(x) = w] \leq \exp(\epsilon\|x - x'\|)\mathsf{Pr}[\mathcal{A}(x') = w]$. Since the above argument holds for all x, x' simultaneously, we get the $\mathcal{A}$ is (ϵ, δ)-Lipschitz private.

Since Algorithm PRIVEMB can be viewed as applying the above mechanism $\mathcal{A}$ on the $x_1, \dots, x_n$ independently, we get that Algorithm PRIVEMB is (ϵ, δ)-Lipschitz private. □

Proposition 13 (Proposition 7 Restated)**.** *Consider Algorithm* PRIVEMB*. With probability at least $1-\delta$, for all pairs $x_i, x_j \in (x_1, \dots, x_n)$, $|\|w_i - w_j\| - \|x_i - x_j\|| \leq 2\beta\tau + 4(m\ln(2nm/\delta))/\epsilon$.*

Proof. Let $w_i = \Phi x_i + \kappa_i$ and $w_j = \Phi x_j + \kappa_j$. Using Theorem 1, with probability at least $1-\delta$,

$$\begin{aligned}&|\|w_i - w_j\| - \|x_i - x_j\|| \\ &= |\|\Phi x_i + \kappa_i - (\Phi x_j + \kappa_j)\| - \|x_i - x_j\|| \\ &\leq |\|\Phi(x_i - x_j)\| - \|x_i - x_j\| + \|\kappa_i\| + \|\kappa_j\|| \\ &\leq \beta\|x_i - x_j\| + \|\kappa_i\| + \|\kappa_j\|. \qquad (2)\end{aligned}$$

For a fixed i, from Claim 6, we get that with probability at least $1-\delta$, $\|\kappa_i\| \leq (2m\ln(m/\delta))/\epsilon$. Using a union bound,

$$\mathsf{Pr}[\forall i \in [n], \|\kappa_i\| \leq (2m\ln(nm/\delta))/\epsilon] \geq 1 - \delta.$$

Plugging this into (2), we get that with probability at least $1 - 2\delta$, for all $i, j \in [n]$

$$|\|w_i - w_j\| - \|x_i - x_j\|| \leq \beta\|x_i - x_j\| + 4(m\ln(nm/\delta))/\epsilon.$$

Using $\|x_i - x_j\| \leq 2\tau$ and scaling δ completes the proof. □

Proposition 14 (Proposition 8 Restated)**.** *Consider Algorithm* PRIVEMB*. With probability at least $1-\delta$, for all pairs $x_i, x_j \in (x_1, \dots, x_n)$, $|\langle w_i, w_j\rangle - \langle x_i, x_j\rangle| \leq \beta\tau^2 + 8\tau m\ln(2nm/\delta)/\epsilon + (2m\ln(2nm/\delta))^2/\epsilon^2$.*

Proof. Let $w_i = \Phi x_i + \kappa_i$ and $w_j = \Phi x_j + \kappa_j$. Using Corollary 2, with probability at least $1-\delta$,

$$\begin{aligned}&|\langle w_i, w_j\rangle - \langle x_i, x_j\rangle| \\ &= |\langle \Phi x_i + \kappa_i, \Phi x_j + \kappa_j\rangle - \langle x_i, x_j\rangle| \\ &= |\langle \Phi x_i, \Phi x_j\rangle + \langle \Phi x_i, \kappa_j\rangle + \langle \kappa_i, \Phi x_j\rangle + \langle \kappa_i, \kappa_j\rangle - \langle x_i, x_j\rangle| \\ &\leq \beta\|x_i\|x_j\| + |\langle \Phi x_i, \kappa_j\rangle + \langle \kappa_i, \Phi x_j\rangle + \langle \kappa_i, \kappa_j\rangle| \\ &\leq \beta\|x_i\|x_j\| + (1+\beta)\|x_i\|\|\kappa_j\| + (1+\beta)\|x_j\|\|\kappa_i\| + \|\kappa_i\|\|\kappa_j\| \\ &\leq \beta\tau^2 + 2\tau(\|\kappa_j\| + \|\kappa_i\|) + \|\kappa_i\|\|\kappa_j\|. \qquad (3)\end{aligned}$$

As in Proposition 7,

$$\mathsf{Pr}[\forall i \in [n], \|\kappa_i\| \leq (2m\ln(nm/\delta))/\epsilon] \geq 1 - \delta.$$

Plugging this into (3), we get that with probability at least $1 - 2\delta$, for all $i, j \in [n]$

$$|\langle w_i, w_j\rangle - \langle x_i, x_j\rangle| \leq \beta\tau^2 + \frac{8\tau m\ln(nm/\delta)}{\epsilon} + \frac{(2m\ln(nm/\delta))^2}{\epsilon^2}.$$

By scaling δ we get the claimed bound. □

Proposition 15 (Proposition 9 Restated)**.** *Consider Algorithm* PRIVEMB*. With probability at least $1-\delta$,*

$$\begin{aligned}\min_{\theta \in \Theta} \frac{1}{n}\sum_{i=1}^{n} \ell(\langle w_i, \Phi\theta\rangle; y_i) &\leq \frac{1}{n}\sum_{i=1}^{n} \ell(\langle x_i, \theta^\star\rangle; y_i) \\ &+ \frac{4\lambda_\ell(m\ln(2nm/\delta))\|\Theta\|}{\epsilon} + \lambda_\ell\beta\tau\|\Theta\|.\end{aligned}$$

Proof. By the Lipschitzness assumption,

$$\begin{aligned}&|\ell(\langle w_i, \Phi\theta^\star\rangle; y_i) - \ell(\langle x_i, \theta^\star\rangle; y_i)| \\ &\leq \lambda_\ell|\langle w_i, \Phi\theta^\star\rangle - \langle x_i, \theta^\star\rangle|. \qquad (4)\end{aligned}$$

Focusing on the right hand side, from Corollary 2, with probability at least $1-\delta$, for all $i \in [n]$,

$$\begin{aligned}&|\langle w_i, \Phi\theta^\star\rangle - \langle x_i, \theta^\star\rangle| \\ &= |\langle \Phi x_i + \kappa_i, \Phi\theta^\star\rangle - \langle x_i, \theta^\star\rangle| \\ &\leq |\langle \kappa_i, \Phi\theta^\star\rangle| + \beta\|x_i\|\|\theta^\star\| \\ &\leq (1+\beta)\|\kappa_i\|\|\theta^\star\| + \beta\|x_i\|\|\theta^\star\| \\ &\leq 2\|\kappa_i\|\|\Theta\| + \beta\tau\|\Theta\|,\end{aligned}$$

where we used $\beta \in (0,1)$, $\|x_i\| \leq \tau$, $\|\theta^\star\| \leq \|\Theta\|$, and with probability at least $1-\delta$, $\|\Phi\theta^\star\| \leq (1+\beta)\|\theta^\star\|$ (from Theorem 1). Using the bound on $\|\kappa_i\|$, we get that with probability at least $1-\delta$, for all $i \in [n]$,

$$|\langle w_i, \Phi\theta^\star\rangle - \langle x_i, \theta^\star\rangle| \leq \frac{4(m\ln(2nm/\delta))\|\Theta\|}{\epsilon} + \beta\tau\|\Theta\|.$$

Plugging this into (4) and averaging over i gives that with probability at least $1-\delta$,

$$\frac{1}{n}\sum_{i=1}^{n} \ell(\langle w_i, \Phi\theta^\star\rangle; y_i)$$
$$\leq \frac{1}{n}\sum_{i=1}^{n} \ell(\langle x_i, \theta^\star\rangle; y_i) + \frac{4\lambda_\ell(m\ln(2nm/\delta))\|\Theta\|}{\epsilon} + \lambda_\ell\beta\tau\|\Theta\|.$$

Since,

$$\min_{\theta\in\Theta} \frac{1}{n}\sum_{i=1}^{n} \ell(\langle w_i, \Phi\theta\rangle; y_i) \leq \frac{1}{n}\sum_{i=1}^{n} \ell(\langle w_i, \Phi\theta^\star\rangle; y_i),$$

we get the claimed result. □

Accountable Error Characterization

Amita Misra, Zhe Liu and Jalal Mahmud
IBM-Research, Almaden
San Jose, CA, USA
amita.misra1|liuzh|jumahmud@ibm.com

Abstract

Customers of machine learning systems demand accountability from the companies employing these algorithms for various prediction tasks. Accountability requires understanding of system limit and condition of erroneous predictions, as customers are often interested in understanding the incorrect predictions, and model developers are absorbed in finding methods that can be used to get incremental improvements to an existing system. Therefore, we propose an accountable error characterization method, AEC, to understand when and where errors occur within the existing black-box models. AEC, as constructed with human-understandable linguistic features, allows the model developers to automatically identify the main sources of errors for a given classification system. It can also be used to sample for the set of most informative input points for a next round of training. We perform error detection for a sentiment analysis task using AEC as a case study. Our results on the sample sentiment task show that AEC is able to characterize erroneous predictions into human understandable categories and also achieves promising results on selecting erroneous samples when compared with the uncertainty-based sampling.

1 Introduction

As machine learning is becoming the method of choice for many analytics functionalities in industry, it becomes crucial to be able to understand the limits and risks of the existing models. In favour of more accurate AI, the availability of computational resources is coupled with increasing dataset sizes that has resulted in more complex models. Complex models suffer from lack of transparency, which leads to low trust as well as the inability to fix or improve the models output easily. Deep learning algorithms are among the highly accurate and complex models. Most users of deep learning models often treat them as a black box because of its incomprehensible functions and unclear working mechanism (Liu et al., 2019). However, customers' retention requires accountability for these systems (Galitsky, 2018). Interpreting and understanding what the model has learned, as well as the limits and the risks of the existing model have therefore become a key ingredient of a robust validation (Montavon et al., 2018).

One line of research on model accountability examines the information learned by the model itself to probe the linguistic aspects of language learnt by the models (Shi et al., 2016; Adi et al., 2017; Giulianelli et al., 2018; Belinkov and Glass, 2019; Liu et al., 2019). Other line of research gives machine learning models the ability to explain or to present their behaviours in understandable terms to humans (Doshi-Velez and Kim, 2017) to make the predictions more transparent, and trustworthy. However, very few studies set the focus on error characterization as well as automatic error detection and mitigation. To address the above-mentioned gaps in characterizing model limits and risks, we seek to improve a model's behavior by categorizing incorrect predictions using explainable linguistic features. To accomplish that, we propose a framework called Accountable Error Characterization (AEC) to explain the predictions of a neural network model by constructing an explainable error classifier. The most similar work to ours is by (Nushi et al., 2018). They build interpretable decision-tree classifiers for summarizing failure conditions using human and machine generated features. In contrast, our approach builds upon incorrect predictions on a separate set to provide insights into model failure.

The AEC framework has three key components: A base neural network model, an error characterization model, and a set of interpretable features that serve as the input to the error characterization model. The features used in the error characterization model are based on explainable linguistic and lexical features such as dependency relations, and

Proceedings of the First Workshop on Trustworthy Natural Language Processing, pages 28–33
June 10, 2021.

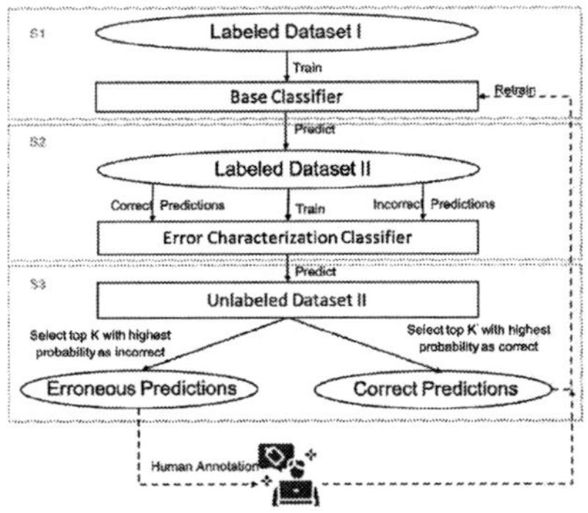

Figure 1: The overall workflow of AEC. Dashed lines represent planned future work

various lexicons that have been inspired by prior art, which allows the users and model developers to identify when a model fails. The error characterization model also offer rankings of informative features to provide insight into where and why the model fails.

By adding the error classification step on top of the base model, AEC can also be adopted to identify the highly confident error cases as the most informative samples for the next round of training. Although uncertainty based sampling can also be adopted to get the most informative samples (Lewis, 1995; Cawley, 2011; Shao et al., 2019), as it selects the examples with the least confidence, Ghai et al. (2020) show that uncertainty sampling led to an increasing challenge for annotators to provide correct labels. AEC avoids such problem by learning from error cases from a validation set. Our results show that AEC outperforms the uncertainty based sampling in terms of selecting erroneous predictions on a sample sentiment dataset (see Table 4).

We first present the overall framework of AEC to construct the error classifier, followed by the experiments and result. Finally, we conclude the paper with future directions and work in progress.

2 Explainable Framework

Figure 1 summarizes our overall method for constructing a human understandable classifier that can be used to explain the erroneous predictions of a deep neural network classifier and thus to improve the model performance. Our method consists of the following steps:

S1: Train a neural network based classifier using labeled dataset I, call it as the base classifier.

S2: Apply the base classifier on another labeled dataset II to get correct and incorrect prediction cases, based on which train a second 2-class error identification classifier with a set of human understandable features. Note here labeled dataset I and II can be in the same domain or in different domains.

S3: Rank the features according to their individual predictive power. Apply the error identification classifier from step 2, to a set of unlabeled data from the same domain as labeled dataset II and rank the unlabeled instances according to their prediction probability of being erroneous. These represent the most informative samples that can be further used in an active learning setting.

The focus of the current work is to identify and characterize the error cases of a base classifier in an human understandable manner. The following two sections describe the experiments and implementation of the framework using a sentiment prediction task as case study. The integration of these samples into an iterative training set up is a work in progress for future extension.

3 Machine Learning Experiments and Results

3.1 Data

We adopt a cross-domain sentiment analysis task as case study in this section to demonstrate the AEC method, although the proposed method would also be applicable to datasets from the same domain. We chose the cross-domain sentiment analysis task here as it is a challenging, but necessary task within the NLP domain and there are high chances of observing erroneous predictions. We use data from two different domains, Stanford Sentiment Treebank (SST) (Socher et al., 2013) (Labeled Dataset I) to train the base classifier, and a conversational Kaggle Airlines dataset (Labeled + Unlabeled Dataset II) to build and evaluate the error characterization classifier. The conversation domain represents a new dataset seeking an improvement on the base classifier trained using sentiment reviews.

SST dataset: A dataset of movie reviews annotated at 5 levels (very negative, negative, neutral, positive, and very positive). Sentence level annotations are extracted using the python package *pytree-*

DataSet	Negative	Neutral	Positive
SST	3304	1622	3605

Table 1: SST dataset distribution

DataSet	Negative	Neutral	Positive
Airline	7366	2451	1847

Table 2: Airline dataset distribution

bank [1]. We merged the *negative and very-negative* class labels into a single negative class, *positive and very-positive* into a single positive class, keeping neutral as it is. A preprocessing step to remove near duplicates gives a training set distribution as shown in Table 1. This is the only dataset used to train the base classifier.

Twitter Airline Dataset: The dataset is available through the library *Crowdflower's Data for Everyone.* [2] Each tweet is classified as either positive, neutral, or negative. The label distribution for the Twitter Airline is shown in Table 2.

3.2 Train the Base Classifier

We chose Convolution Neural Network (CNN) as a showcase here, as the base sentiment classifier to be trained using the SST dataset. However, the framework can be easily adapted to more advanced state of the art classifiers such as BERT (Devlin et al., 2019). A multi-channel CNN architecture is employed to train as it has been shown to work well on multiple sentiment datasets including SST (Kim, 2014). The samples are weighted to account for class imbalance.

3.3 Train the Error Characterization Classifier

We next applied the trained base classifier on the training set of a cross-domain dataset as described in Table 2 to get the predictions on a sample of 11664 labeled instances of Airlines dataset. Predictions from the base model on this Airlines dataset are further divided into two classes based on the ground truth test labels, correct-prediction and incorrect-prediction. The base classifier has an overall accuracy of 60.09% on the Airline dataset as shown in Table 3. A balanced set is created by undersampling the correct predictions giving a dataset of total 9310 instances. We use a 80/20 split for training and testing giving a training set of 7448 and a test set of 1862 instances. This train set serves as the input to train the error characterization classifier with erroneous or not as labels and different collections of explainable features as independent variables. A random forest classifier using a 5-fold cross validation was used to train the error characterization classifier. (Pedregosa et al., 2011).

Dataset	Total instances	Correct pred.	InCorrect pred.
Airline dataset	11664	7009	4655

Table 3: Performance of the Base classifier on the Airline dataset

3.3.1 Features

Our features have been inspired by previous work on sentiment, disagreement, and conversations. The feature values are normalized by sentence length.

Generalized Dependency. Dependency relations are obtained using the python package *spacy* [3]. Relations are generalized by replacing the words in each dependency relation by their corresponding POS tag (Joshi and Penstein-Rosé, 2009; Abbott et al., 2011; Misra et al., 2016).

Emotion. Count of words in each of the 8 emotion classes from the NRC emotion lexicon (anger, anticipation, disgust, fear, joy, negative, positive, sadness, surprise, and trust) available from (Mohammad and Turney, 2010).

Named Entities. The count of named entities of each entity type obtained from the python package spacy.

Conversation. Lexical indicators indicating greetings, thank, apology, second person reference, questions starting with do, did, can, could, with who, what, where as described by (Oraby et al., 2017).

3.4 Predict erroneous predictions from unlabeled data

Once the error characterization classifier was trained with the set of correctly and incorrectly predicted instances, we then apply it to the 20% test set of the Twitter Airline data, which consists of a total of 1862 instances as described in section 3.3. We selected the top K instances with the highest probability of being incorrectly predicted as the erroneous cases. We hide the actual labels on this

[1] https://pypi.org/project/pytreebank

[2] https://appen.com/resources/datasets/

[3] https://spacy.io

test set when selecting the instances. The actual labels will be later used to evaluate the performance of the error characterization classifier.

4 Evaluation and Results

In terms of identifying erroneous predictions, in our evaluation, we compare the performance of AEC with uncertainty-based sampling, in which the learner computes a probabilistic output for each sample, and select the samples that the base classifier is the most uncertain about based on probability scores.

4.1 Most informative samples for labeling.

As we are interested in generating a ranking of incorrect predictions for the base classifier from error characterization classifier, we use *precision at top k* as the evaluation metrics in here, which is a commonly used metric in information retrieval, and defined as P@K=N/K, where N is the actual number of errors samples among top K predicted. We compare the performance of the error characterization classifier and the uncertainty based sampling on the test set of 1832 instances as shown in Table 4. It shows the precision at top K where K varies from 10 to 50. For the first initial 10 samples, the uncertainty based sampling performs marginally better but as we select more samples (rows 2-5) the proposed approach starts outperforming the baseline.

TOP K	uncertainty-based P@K	AEC P@K
10	0.8	0.7
20	0.75	0.8
30	0.77	0.83
40	0.75	0.83
50	0.74	0.76

Table 4: Comparison of uncertainty-based sampling (Baseline) with proposed AEC on the test set.

4.2 Feature Characterization

When using uncertainity based sampling, it is not always evident why certain samples were selected, or how these samples map to actual errors of the base classifier. In contrast, AEC framework incorporates explainability into sample selection by mapping highly ranked feature sets from the error characterization model with the selected error samples.

S.No	Text	Base Pred.	Actual Label	Error. Prob
1	@username**if you could** change your name to @southwestair and **do what** they do...that'd be **awesome**. Also this plane **smells** like onion rings.	Neutral	Negative	0.84
2	@username now on hold for **90 minutes**	Neutral	Negative	0.82
3	@username user is a **compassionate** professional! Despite the flight challenges she made passengers feel like priorities!!	Neutral	Positive	0.79

Table 5: A subset of most informative samples for the Base classifier based on error characterization classifier probability score for the error class.

Table 5 shows a few examples of actual errors from the base classifier that are also predicted to be errors on the test set from the error characterization classifier. Words in bold show a few of these feature mappings. For example, feature set of Row-1 has higher values for the feature *question-starters*, text of Row-3 contains *Named Entity type: time,* a feature present in highly ranked feature-set of the error characterization classifier as shown in Table 6.

Feature Type	Highly ranked features
Lexical	second_person, question_yesno, question_wh !, ?,thanks, no
NRC	positive, negative, trust, fear, anger,
Entities	Org, Time , Date, Cardinal
Dependency	amod-NN-JJ, nummod-NNS,CD, compound-NN-NN, ROOT-NNP-NNP, advmod-VB-RB compound-NN-NNP, neg-VB-RB, amod-NNS,JJ, ROOT-VBN-VBN

Table 6: A subset of top 100 Features from Random Forest.

5 Conclusion and Future Work

We present an error characterization framework, called AEC, which allows the model users and developers to understand when and where a model fails. AEC is trained on human understandable linguistic features with erroneous predictions from the base classifier as training input. We used a cross-domain sentiment analysis task as case study to showcase the effectiveness of AEC in terms of error detection and characterization. Our experiments showed that AEC outperformed uncertainty based sampling in terms of selecting the erroneous samples for continuous model improvements (a strong active learning baseline for selecting the most uncertain samples for continuous model improvements) for the task of predicting errors which can act as most informative samples of the base classifier. In addition, errors automatically detected by AEC seemed to be more understandable to the model developers. Having these explanations lets the end users make a more informed decision, as well as guide the labeling decisions for next round of training. As our initial results on sentiment dataset look promising for both performance and explainability, we are in the process of extending the framework to run the algorithm iteratively on multiple datasets. While applying the error characterization classifier on the unlabeled datasets, not only we will select the top K' instances with the highest prediction probability of being correctly predicted and add them back to the original training dataset for retraining purpose, but we will also select top K instances with the highest prediction probability of being incorrectly predicted. We will assign those instances to human annotators for labels and add them back to the original labeled data as well for the next iteration of training process. We will continuously feed these samples to train the base network, and evaluate the actual performance gains for the base classifier.

References

Rob Abbott, Marilyn Walker, Jean E. Fox Tree, Pranav Anand, Robeson Bowmani, and Joseph King. 2011. How can you say such things?!?: Recognizing Disagreement in Informal Political Argument. In *Proc. of the ACL Workshop on Language and Social Media*.

Yossi Adi, Einat Kermany, Yonatan Belinkov, Ofer Lavi, and Yoav Goldberg. 2017. Fine-grained analysis of sentence embeddings using auxiliary prediction tasks. In *5th International Conference on Learning Representations, ICLR 2017, Toulon, France, April 24-26, 2017, Conference Track Proceedings*. OpenReview.net.

Yonatan Belinkov and James Glass. 2019. Analysis methods in neural language processing: A survey. *Transactions of the Association for Computational Linguistics*, 7:49–72.

Gavin C. Cawley. 2011. Baseline methods for active learning. In *Active Learning and Experimental Design workshop, In conjunction with AISTATS 2010, Sardinia, Italy, May 16, 2010*, volume 16 of *JMLR Proceedings*, pages 47–57. JMLR.org.

Jacob Devlin, Ming-Wei Chang, Kenton Lee, and Kristina Toutanova. 2019. BERT: pre-training of deep bidirectional transformers for language understanding. In *Proceedings of the 2019 Conference of the North American Chapter of the Association for Computational Linguistics: Human Language Technologies, NAACL-HLT 2019, Minneapolis, MN, USA, June 2-7, 2019, Volume 1 (Long and Short Papers)*, pages 4171–4186. Association for Computational Linguistics.

Finale Doshi-Velez and Been Kim. 2017. Towards a rigorous science of interpretable machine learning. *arXiv: Machine Learning*.

Boris Galitsky. 2018. Customers' retention requires an explainability feature in machine learning systems they use. In *2018 AAAI Spring Symposia, Stanford University, Palo Alto, California, USA, March 26-28, 2018*. AAAI Press.

Bhavya Ghai, Q. Vera Liao, Yunfeng Zhang, Rachel K. E. Bellamy, and Klaus Mueller. 2020. Explainable active learning (XAL): toward AI explanations as interfaces for machine teachers. *Proc. ACM Hum. Comput. Interact.*, 4(CSCW3):1–28.

Mario Giulianelli, Jack Harding, Florian Mohnert, Dieuwke Hupkes, and Willem H. Zuidema. 2018. Under the hood: Using diagnostic classifiers to investigate and improve how language models track agreement information. In *Proceedings of the Workshop: Analyzing and Interpreting Neural Networks for NLP, BlackboxNLP EMNLP 2018, Brussels, Belgium, November 1, 2018*, pages 240–248. Association for Computational Linguistics.

M. Joshi and C. Penstein-Rosé. 2009. Generalizing dependency features for opinion mining. In *Proc. of the ACL-IJCNLP 2009 Conference Short Papers*, pages 313–316.

Yoon Kim. 2014. Convolutional neural networks for sentence classification. In *Proceedings of the 2014 Conference on Empirical Methods in Natural Language Processing, EMNLP 2014, October 25-29, 2014, Doha, Qatar, A meeting of SIGDAT, a Special Interest Group of the ACL*, pages 1746–1751.

David D. Lewis. 1995. A sequential algorithm for training text classifiers: Corrigendum and additional data. *SIGIR Forum*, 29(2):13–19.

Hui Liu, Qingyu Yin, and William Yang Wang. 2019. Towards explainable NLP: A generative explanation framework for text classification. In *Proceedings of the 57th Conference of the Association for Computational Linguistics, ACL 2019, Florence, Italy, July 28- August 2, 2019, Volume 1: Long Papers*, pages 5570–5581. Association for Computational Linguistics.

Amita Misra, Brian Ecker, and Marilyn A. Walker. 2016. Measuring the similarity of sentential arguments in dialogue. In *Proceedings of the SIGDIAL 2016 Conference, The 17th Annual Meeting of the Special Interest Group on Discourse and Dialogue, 13-15 September 2016, Los Angeles, CA, USA*, pages 276–287. The Association for Computer Linguistics.

Saif M Mohammad and Peter D Turney. 2010. Emotions evoked by common words and phrases: Using mechanical turk to create an emotion lexicon. In *Proceedings of the NAACL HLT 2010 workshop on computational approaches to analysis and generation of emotion in text*, pages 26–34. Association for Computational Linguistics.

Grégoire Montavon, Wojciech Samek, and Klaus-Robert Müller. 2018. Methods for interpreting and understanding deep neural networks. *Digit. Signal Process.*, 73:1–15.

Besmira Nushi, Ece Kamar, and Eric Horvitz. 2018. Towards accountable AI: hybrid human-machine analyses for characterizing system failure. In *Proceedings of the Sixth AAAI Conference on Human Computation and Crowdsourcing, HCOMP 2018, Zürich, Switzerland, July 5-8, 2018*, pages 126–135. AAAI Press.

Shereen Oraby, Pritam Gundecha, Jalal Mahmud, Mansurul Bhuiyan, and Rama Akkiraju. 2017. "how may I help you?": Modeling twitter customer serviceconversations using fine-grained dialogue acts. In *Proceedings of the 22nd International Conference on Intelligent User Interfaces, IUI 2017, Limassol, Cyprus, March 13-16, 2017*, pages 343–355. ACM.

F. Pedregosa, G. Varoquaux, A. Gramfort, V. Michel, B. Thirion, O. Grisel, M. Blondel, P. Prettenhofer, R. Weiss, V. Dubourg, J. Vanderplas, A. Passos, D. Cournapeau, M. Brucher, M. Perrot, and E. Duchesnay. 2011. Scikit-learn: Machine learning in Python. *Journal of Machine Learning Research*, 12:2825–2830.

Jingyu Shao, Qing Wang, and Fangbing Liu. 2019. Learning to sample: An active learning framework. In *2019 IEEE International Conference on Data Mining, ICDM 2019, Beijing, China, November 8-11, 2019*, pages 538–547. IEEE.

Xing Shi, Inkit Padhi, and Kevin Knight. 2016. Does string-based neural MT learn source syntax? In *Proceedings of the 2016 Conference on Empirical Methods in Natural Language Processing*. Association for Computational Linguistics.

Richard Socher, Alex Perelygin, Jean Wu, Jason Chuang, Christopher D. Manning, Andrew Ng, and Christopher Potts. 2013. Recursive deep models for semantic compositionality over a sentiment treebank. In *Proc. of the 2013 Conference on Empirical Methods in Natural Language Processing*, pages 1631–1642.

xER: An Explainable Model for Entity Resolution using an Efficient Solution for the Clique Partitioning Problem

Samhita Vadrevu
University of Illinois
at Urbana-Champaign
samhita3@illinois.edu

Wen-Mei Hwu
University of Illinois
at Urbana-Champaign
w-hwu@illinois.edu

Rakesh Nagi
University of Illinois
at Urbana-Champaign
nagi@illinois.edu

Jinjun Xiong
IBM T. J. Watson Research Center
Yorktown Heights, NY, USA
jinjun@us.ibm.com

Abstract

In this paper, we propose a global, self-explainable solution to solve a prominent NLP problem: Entity Resolution (ER). We formulate ER as a graph partitioning problem. Every mention of a real-world entity is represented by a node in the graph, and the pairwise similarity scores between the mentions are used to associate these nodes to exactly one clique, which represents a real-world entity in the ER domain. In this paper, we use Clique Partitioning Problem (CPP), which is an Integer Program (IP) to formulate ER as a graph partitioning problem and then highlight the explainable nature of this method. Since CPP is NP-Hard, we introduce an efficient solution procedure, the **xER** algorithm, to solve CPP as a combination of finding maximal cliques in the graph and then performing *generalized* set packing using a novel formulation. We discuss the advantages of using xER over the traditional methods and provide the computational experiments and results of applying this method to ER data sets.

1 Introduction

Entity Resolution (ER) is a prominent NLP problem, also referred to as co-reference resolution, de-duplication and record linkage, depending on the the problem set up. Irrespective of the name, the objective is to combine and cluster multiple mentions of a real-world entity from various data sources into their respective real-world entities and remove duplicates. Various techniques such as clustering (Aslam et al., 2004), (Saeedi et al., 2017), rule-based methods (Aumüller and Rahm, 2009), mathematical programming, and combinatorial optimization (Tauer et al., 2019) have previously been applied to ER. In this paper, we formulate and solve ER as a graph partitioning problem.

Representing ER as a graph partitioning problem The transformation from the real-world ER problem domain to the mathematical Integer Programming (IP) formulation setup is essential to understand the model's explainable nature and the solution procedure. A node in the graph represents a mention in the ER domain. An edge between any two nodes has a weight associated with it, representing the similarity score between the two mentions in consideration. This similarity score indicates the probability that these mentions are associated with the same entity. The goal is to ensure that based on the weights, the nodes are optimally allotted to their respective clusters. From a combinatorial perspective, this problem is known as the Clique Partitioning Problem (CPP). A clique is a complete subgraph in which all its nodes are pairwise connected. The weight of a clique is defined as the sum of all its edges' weights. The objective of this mathematical formulation is to find disjoint cliques in the graph such that the total weight of all the cliques is maximized, which, in the ER domain, translates to associating each mention to a single real-world entity with the highest probability association. The constraints in this mathematical formulation enforce that a particular node is mapped to just one clique and ensure that the mentions' transitivity conditions are obeyed.

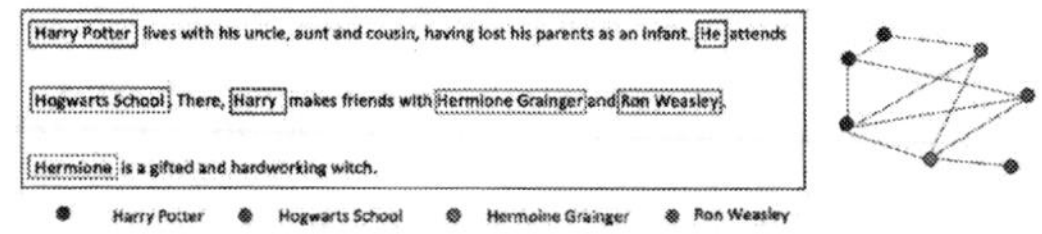

Figure 1: An example of converting a text into a graph.

Bhattacharya and Getoor (2004) was one of the earlier papers that formulated ER as a graphical problem and Bansal et al. (2004) proposed a correlation clustering method for the graphical problem. ER was also approached as a graph partitioning problem in (Nicolae and Nicolae, 2006), (Chen and Ji, 2009), (Chen and Ji, 2010) and the CPP approach outperformed other solution methods for

Proceedings of the First Workshop on Trustworthy Natural Language Processing, pages 34–44
June 10, 2021.

ER (Finkel et al., 2005), (Klenner and Ailloud, 2009). Tauer et al. (2019) formulated ER as CPP, where an incremental graph partitioning approach was applied and solved using a heuristic. Lokhande et al. (2020) formulated ER as a set packing problem by considering the sets of all possible combinations of mentions and then choosing the best combination, based on the weights of the sets. ER has also been approached as a clustering problem. Saeedi et al. (2017) conducted an extensive survey on the clustering methods that had been applied to the entity resolution problem. von Luxburg (2007) solved ER as a spectral graph clustering problem, which is based on the graph's Laplacian matrix. Star Clustering (Aslam et al., 2004) formalizes clustering as graph covering and assigns each node to the highest probabilistic cluster. k-means is also a common technique to solve ER as a clustering problem. However, the mathematical formulation based methods come with a guarantee of optimality. Furthermore, it is easy to obtain an upper bound to these problems by relaxing the integer constraints. These upper bounds provide a guarantee on any feasible solution. In typical clustering algorithms, the number of clusters to produce in the output needs to be provided upfront, while it is decided by the model intrinsically in the CPP framework. The long convergence times and the iterations pose a disadvantage for them to be used as a solution technique for entity resolution (Saeedi et al., 2017). Moreover, from an explainability perspective, in the formulation-based methods proposed in this paper, the explanation is substantiated with mathematical guarantees, while the clustering-based approaches lack this mathematical precision and the heuristic nature further confounds explainability. Ribeiro et al. (2016), Ribeiro et al. (2018), Letham et al. (2015) and Choudhary et al. (2018) have proposed explainable systems for ER using local and if-then-else based global explanations. Ebaid et al. (2019) is a tool that provides explanations at different granularity levels.

Since CPP is NP-hard (Grötschel and Wakabayashi, 1989), a novel two-phase solution is proposed, in this paper, to solve CPP optimally. This solution method can be easily accelerated and scaled to handle large-sized datasets. As a part of this two-phased approach, new and creative formulations for the generalized set packing problem are also proposed. The formulations and the approach to obtain the optimal solution provide a mathematical guarantee on the output, and the results are easily interpretable and explainable. The constraints and objective function mathematically support the explanation behind the predicted output.

The rest of the paper is organized as follows. In Section 2, entity resolution is formulated as CPP. In Section 3, explainability and interpretability of this method is discussed. Section 4 then introduces the two-phase solution approach proposed for solving the NP-hard CPP. Sections 5 and 6 go over the computational experiments and the results.

2 Mathematical Formulation of CPP

As discussed in Section 1, the entity resolution problem is transformed to a graph where each mention is represented by nodes and the weight on an edge between the nodes is the similarity score between the mentions. To obtain the pairwise similarity scores, we use an open-source entity resolution library called Dedupe (Gregg and Eder, 2019), which applies blocking and a logistic regression based model to obtain the similarity scores between mentions. See Section 5 for more details about this.

In this section, the graph partitioning setup is formally represented by a mathematical formulation. Let i, j $(i < j)$ be two nodes in the graph (representing two mentions) and w_{ij} be the weight of the edge between these nodes. x_{ij} is a binary variable that denotes whether i, j are associated or co-referent (belong to the same clique).

$$x_{ij} = \begin{cases} 1 \text{ if nodes } i, j \text{ are associated} \\ 0 \text{ otherwise} \end{cases}$$

The "traditional" math formulation of CPP is:

$$CPP(\boldsymbol{w}) = \max \sum_{i=1}^{N-1} \sum_{j=i+1}^{N} w_{ij} x_{ij}; \ \ s.t. \tag{1}$$

$$x_{ij} + x_{ik} - x_{jk} \leq 1, \ \ \forall 1 \leq i < j < k \leq N, \tag{2}$$

$$-x_{ij} + x_{ik} + x_{jk} \leq 1, \ \ \forall 1 \leq i < j < k \leq N, \tag{3}$$

$$x_{ij} - x_{ik} + x_{jk} \leq 1, \ \ \forall 1 \leq i < j < k \leq N, \tag{4}$$

$$x_{ij} \in \{0, 1\}, \ \ \forall 1 \leq i < j \leq N. \tag{5}$$

Constraints (2), (3), and (4) are the transitivity constraints enforced among the nodes. These three constraints ensure that if mention a is the same as b and b is the same as c, then it must also be that a is the same as c. The graph is assumed to be directed to avoid duplication of cliques and memory exhaustion. An optimal solution to this problem results in the best possible solution to the ER for the given similarity scores. However, due to cubic number of constraints, this particular formulation for CPP, does not scale with the number of nodes. Hence, heuristics are prevalent to find an approximate solution to CPP; see Section 4 for details.

3 Model Explainability and Interpretability

Before we discuss our solution approaches, the explainable nature of this method is highlighted. The definitions of explainability have been studied in various works (Guidotti et al., 2019), (Arya et al., 2019). As defined in Danilevsky et al. (2020) and Guidotti et al. (2019), understanding the level of explainability of models can be interpreted as *outcome explanation problems*, where the emphasis lies in understanding the rationale behind the prediction of a specific output or all outputs in general. In this paper, the definitions and categorizations of explanations are based on the definitions in Danilevsky et al. (2020). Two major categorizations of explanations are emphasized. The first is based on the explanation process's target set, and divided into two types: Local and Global. Suppose the explanation is for a particular individual output. In that case, the explanation type is referred to as *Local*. On the other hand, if the explanation is for the whole model in itself, then it is a *Global* explanation. The second categorization is based on the origin of the explanation process. If the explanation is from the prediction process itself, then it belongs to the *Self Explaining* or the *Directly Interpretable* category (Arya et al., 2019). Otherwise, if post prediction processing is required to explain the output, it can be categorized as *Post-hoc* explanation.

As seen in Tauer et al. (2019), mathematical formulation based methods have a notion of optimality infused in the problems. The design of NLP problems like ER as mathematical formulations ensures that various constraints are met simultaneously, and hence making the output and the prediction process trustworthy and reliable. Since the constraints and the objective function are enforced into the mathematical formulation, the explanation behind any output comes directly from the model itself, making it a self-explainable model model. Moreover, the explanation behind any output is only dependent on the formulation and not on the output itself. This makes the model globally explainable. Therefore, by applying an efficient approach based on mathematical formulations, the solution method discussed in this paper presents an easily interpretable and explainable model for ER.

4 Solution Approach for CPP

As discussed in Section 2, CPP is NP-hard. In this paper, an efficient and scalable solution approach is proposed to solve the CPP.

The solution procedure is divided into two phases: Phase 1 involves finding the maximal cliques in the graph. A maximal clique is a clique that is not a sub-clique of a larger clique (Akkoyunlu, 1973). For Phase 2, we propose a novel *generalized* set packing formulation that not only ensures that each node belongs to a single clique, but it is able to break larger cliques into smaller sub-cliques if necessary. The formulation enables to find the optimal combinations of the cliques, that maximize the weight of the system. The algorithm (Phase 1 + Phase 2), is referred to as **xER** (Explainable ER).

4.1 Phase 1: Finding Maximal Cliques

In this phase, all the maximal cliques in a graph are found and stored. There are many approaches to find maximal cliques, but the most prominent and efficient approach is the Bron-Kerbosch (BK) algorithm (Bron and Kerbosch, 1973). There are multiple variants of BK, and in this paper, we adopt the pivot-based BK algorithm with node ordering. For simplicity, a recursion-based sequential implementation is used for BK. However, a scalable GPU-accelerated implementation for maximal clique listing is currently in progress based on (Almasri et al., 2021).

4.2 Phase 2: Set Packing

The output of Phase 1 is a list of cliques that are not disjoint. This phase aims to find the optimal combination of these cliques such that the cliques are disjoint and the total weight of all these disjoint cliques is maximized. Thus, Phase 2 is a maximum weighted Set Packing Problem (SPP). The original SPP is formulated as:

$$\text{(SPP)} \quad \max \quad W^T x \tag{6}$$
$$\text{s.t} \quad Ax = 1 \tag{7}$$
$$x \in \{0,1\}. \tag{8}$$

Here, S is the list of sets (cliques) and V is the set of nodes in the graph. W denotes the weight vector, where each entry is the weight of a clique. The binary variable x_t denotes if a set $t \in S$ is chosen or not, $A : V \times S$ is the incidence matrix indicating the presence of a node in a set. $a_{it} \in A$ is 1 if node

$i \in V$ is in the set $t \in S$ and 0, otherwise. The formulation of the original set packing problem is designed to choose the optimal packing of sets that maximizes the system's overall weight. Multiple solution procedures have been developed to solve this set packing problem, and these procedures can be categorized as either exact or approximate algorithms. Rossi and Smriglio (2001) proposed a branch-and-cut approach for solving the SPP. Landete et al. (2013) proposed alternate formulations for SPP in higher dimensions and then added valid inequalities that were facets to the lifted polytope. Kwon et al. (2008) and Kolokolov and Zaozerskaya (2009) also proposed new facets that strengthen the relaxed formulations of SPP. Li et al. (2020) encoded SPP as a maximum weighted independent set and then used a Diversion Local Search based on the Weighted Configuration Checking (DLSWCC) algorithm to solve it. Since SPP is NP-hard (Garey and Johnson, 2009), many heuristics have also been proposed to obtain a solution for SPP in a reasonable amount of time. Rönnqvist (1995) proposed a Lagrangian relaxation based method and Delorme et al. (2004) used a greedy randomized adaptive search procedure (GRASP) to solve SPP. Gandibleux et al. (2004) proposed an ant colony heuristic for SPP.

Lokhande et al. (2020) has recently formulated ER as a set packing problem. All possible combinations of groups of mentions are given as an input to the SPP. Each of these groups is referred to as a hypothesis. Every hypothesis has a weight associated with it, which is computed as the sum of weights on a pair of nodes in that hypothesis. The best combination of the sets is chosen based on the weights. A major drawback of formulating and solving ER as a traditional set packing problem is the huge input size even for considerably small graphs. Table 1 shows a comparison between the number of cliques (|C|) and the number of maximal cliques (|MC|) in small-sized graphs, with number of edges denoted as |E|. The number of maximal cliques is significantly less than the total number of cliques. The number of all the cliques in the graph grows exponentially, much faster than the number of maximal cliques as the graph's size increases. In this paper, our proposed formulation for set packing can break a large set into smaller ones if required. Therefore, it only needs the maximal cliques as an input, contrary to SPP, which requires all the cliques as an input.

Nodes	|E|	|MC|	|C|	Ratio $\lceil \frac{\|C\|}{\|MC\|} \rceil$
38	147	70	528	8
38	203	101	801	8
38	379	433	5619	13
46	223	87	2466	28
46	317	162	3264	20
46	556	829	17114	21

Table 1: Statistics of small graphs and their associated edges.

4.2.1 Proposed SPP Formulation

As discussed in Section 4.2, the formulation of the original set packing problem is designed to choose the combination of sets that are disjoint and maximize the problem's overall weight. Thus, it requires the power set of cliques as an input. In this paper, the traditional set packing formulation is modified to fit the ER problem's requirements and made it more efficient and scalable to handle large datasets. Our novel formulation for set packing is introduced in Section 4.2 requires a much smaller input size. The formulation itself is enabled to carve out sub-cliques of a larger clique while keeping them disjoint. Eventually, the same optimal solution would be found, but the difference is in the manageable input size.

Notation: Here, K is the total number of maximal cliques in the input. Each set of index k, is denoted by S_k (cliques and sets are used interchangeably to accommodate the notation of both the traditional set packing and the new proposed formulation). The inputs to the problem is a set of incidence matrices $\{A_k\}$ corresponding to each set S_k, and W, the weight matrix of arcs in the original graph. The graph is directed, and an edge can only exist between two nodes i, j, with $i < j$ and weight W_{ij}. Each set can be broken down into multiple partitions, and M is the upper bound on the total number of partitions any set can be broken down into. The index for each partition of a set is m and is local to a set S_k, where $0 \leq m \leq M - 1$. z_{ij} denotes the connection between two nodes i, j in the optimal solution and y_{imk} denotes if node i is assigned to partition m of set S_k .

Decision Variables:

$$y_{imk} = \begin{cases} 1 \text{ if node } i \text{ is chosen for partition } m \text{ in set } S_k \\ 0 \text{ otherwise} \end{cases}$$

$$z_{ij} = \begin{cases} 1 \text{ if nodes } i, j \text{ belong to the same partition} \\ 0 \text{ otherwise} \end{cases}$$

All the nodes in V are ordered. E represents the edge set of the graph. $E = \{(i, j) : i < j\}$.

4.2.2 Quadratic Set Packing

The new set packing formulation is as follows:

$$\text{(QSP)}\ \max \sum_{i=0}^{N-1} \sum_{j=i+1}^{N-1} W_{ij} z_{ij};\ \ s.t. \tag{9}$$

$$z_{ij} - \sum_{k} \sum_{m} y_{imk} \times y_{jmk} = 0, \forall i, j \in V, \tag{10}$$

$$\sum_{k} \sum_{m} y_{imk} \leq 1 \qquad \forall i \in V, \tag{11}$$

$$0 \leq z_{ij} \leq 1, y_{imk} \in \{0,1\},\ \ \forall i, j \in V, m \in M, k \in K. \tag{12}$$

QSP stands for Quadratic Set Packing, deriving the name from the quadratic nature of the constraints. It can be observed that the notation of the variables in this formulation is different from the traditional set packing formulation. In the traditional set packing formulation, the decision variable is the binary variable x_t, denoting the presence of a set t in the optimal solution. However, in QSP, the decision variable y_{imk} denotes the presence of a node i in the partition m of set S_k. If a node i from set S_k should belong to partition m, the value of $y_{imk} = 1$ and 0 otherwise. This shows that y_{imk} is modified to remove nodes from the maximal cliques if necessary, eliminating the need to provide the power set of the maximal cliques as an input to the original SPP formulation. As mentioned before, this ordering avoids duplication of nodes and saves memory. Moreover, due to the nature of the formulation, even though z_{ij} is not explicitly assigned to be an integral solution, solving the QSP optimally results in an integer solution for z_{ij}. An off-the-shelf optimization solver, Gurobi (Gurobi Optimization, 2021) was used to solve the problem optimally. z_{ij} is used to compute the precision, recall and the F1 scores.

Algorithm 1: xER Algorithm

Result: Resolved datasets with no duplicate mentions

Step 1 : Perform blocking and compute pairwise similarity scores (§5);

Step 2 : Construct a directed graph with the mentions as nodes and similarity scores as weights on the edges. (§4);

Step 3 : Find maximal cliques in the graph using BK (§4.1);

Step 4 : Perform Set Packing using the QSP formulation (§4);

Step 5 : Use the output of z to compute precision, recall and F1 (§5);

Currently, we are working on developing scalable heuristics for the xER algorithm. As mentioned in Sec 4.1, a GPU accelerated version for Phase 1 is currently in progress based on Almasri et al. (2021). For Phase 2, an accelerated and scalable approach is being developed. The QSP formulation is linearized to provide the Linearized Set Packing (LSP) formulation. We are working on the linear relaxations of LSP and using accelerated computing to solve this and a family of relaxations. Subsequently, one can develop branch-and-bound approaches for solving the integer programming problem to optimality.

5 Computational Experiments

In this section, the xER algorithm's performance is evaluated through experiments on different ER datasets. In this paper, two primary data sources considered: benchmarking datasets (Saeedi et al., 2017) and ECB+ (Cybulska and Vossen, 2014). Datasets from both these sources are used to test the algorithm and analyze the algorithm's performance in terms of the F1 scores, solution times and their potential for scalability. Different blocking and scoring techniques have been applied to both these datasets, and are discussed in detail.

Blocking is a pre-processing technique applied to the datasets. The purpose is to eliminate the need to store similarity scores between those pairs of mentions that are extremely unlikely to being associated to the same entity. This increases the sparsity in the graph, making it easier to process the graph and perform computations. Blocking and similarity score computation techniques are different for different data sources and are discussed below.

5.1 Benchmarking Datasets

Saeedi et al. (2017) provides benchmark datasets, three of which are used in this paper. Table 2 shows the statistics for these benchmarking datasets. An open-source entity resolution library called Dedupe (Gregg and Eder, 2019) is used to preprocess these datasets by applying blocking techniques and generating similarity scores. The blocking technique and the scoring scheme are obtained from the code base of Lokhande et al. (2020). The dataset is divided into training and validation sets, with a split ratio of 50%. Our similarity scores for the benchmark datasets are obtained from the Dedupe library by training a ridge regression model.

5.2 ECB+ Corpus

Event Coreference Bank (ECB) (Bejan and Harabagiu, 2010)) is an event coreference resolu-

Dataset	Entities	Matches	Clusters
patent_example	2379	293785	102
csv_example	3337	6608	1162
settlements	3054	4388	820

Table 2: Statistics of the benchmarking datasets

tion dataset that includes a collection of documents found through Google Search. ECB+ (Cybulska and Vossen, 2014) is an extension of this dataset with newly added documents. Table 3 shows the statistics for this dataset.

The ECB+ dataset comes with the gold standard or the Ground Truth (GT) values used to generate the similarity scores. The ground truth values for two connected (or co-referent) and not connected mentions are $+1$ and -1, respectively. The "synthetic" similarity scores are generated from a normal distribution with a fixed mean and an added noise. If the ground-truth is $+1$ then $\mu = 0.5$ and if it is -1, then $\mu = -0.5$. A variance of 0.3 is added to the generated scores using this distribution. Once the similarity scores are computed, a blocking threshold T is applied to these scores. A pair of mentions with a similarity score less than T is blocked, and the edge between these nodes is removed from the original graph. The mentions in this dataset could belong to the *event* class or the *entity* class. The mention pairs are taken from the same class for the experiments, and xER is indifferent to the class.

Type	Mentions	Chains (clusters)
Event	6833	2741
Entity	8289	2224

Table 3: Statistics of ECB+ datasets

This dataset is broken down into smaller graphs using topic modelling from (Barhom et al., 2019). It facilitated the use of these different sized graphs to experiment with the blocking thresholds, analyze the F1 scores, and understand the xER algorithm's performance.

6 Results

The experiments are performed on an Intel i5 processor with 8GB RAM. The datasets from both sources are preprocessed and converted into graphs given as an input to the xER algorithm. These graphs have mentions as nodes and the pairwise similarity scores as the edges' weight. As shown in the xER algorithm (1), this graph is first passed through Phase 1, which is the Bron-Kerbosch algorithm with pivoting (Bron and Kerbosch, 1973). This step's output is a set of maximal cliques that are not disjoint and passed on to Phase 2 for the set packing step. QSP formulation is modelled using Gurobi (Gurobi Optimization, 2021) and solved optimally. The solution for the z variable from the optimally solved model is used to compute F1 scores. The xER algorithm is applied to all the datasets listed above and is evaluated in terms of F1 scores and computation times, and compared to the other competing algorithms. xER is also compared with the traditional set packing algorithm and the difference in the input sizes between SPP and QSP is highlighted through experiments. Also, to demonstrate the quality of the xER algorithm, the weights on the edges are replaced with Ground Truth (GT) values ($+1$ and -1) instead of similarity scores and tested. This helps in analyzing and confirming the model's consistency and accuracy, irrespective of the method used to compute similarity scores.

6.1 Testing xER on benchmarking datasets

Dedupe is used to perform blocking and compute the similarity scores as mentioned in Section 5.1. First, Dedupe employs specific blocking techniques on the data. A ridge regression model is then trained and used to compute the scores on the validation dataset. The pairwise nodes and the scores are passed on to the xER algorithm, and F1 scores are computed using the solutions from the z variable. These scores are obtained from the code base of (Lokhande et al., 2020) for a fair comparison and the performance of xER is compared with F-MWSP in (Lokhande et al., 2020) and a standard Hierarchical Clustering (HC) approach (Hastie et al., 2009). As mentioned before, M is a hyperparameter, and for these three datasets, we set it to 10. Table 4 shows that xER is at least as good as the other algorithms. For the *settlements* dataset, xER outperforms both F-MWSP and HC. For *csv_example*, xER has the same F1 score as F-MWSP, which is better than that of HC. For *patent_sample*, the F1 score for xER is less than HC and F-MWSP. However, since xER is designed to provide an optimal solution to a graph with a given set of nodes and weights, it is possible that the blocking techniques were too severe or the computational scores were not the best, leading to a lower F1 score. As discussed before, a high-quality blocking technique and similarity scores will lead to high-quality F1 scores, since the xER algorithm is designed to give the best possible solution to a given input. Another comparison factor considered is the size of the input between SPP and QSP. The size of the input cliques required for a traditional set packing based formulation (F-MWSP) is significantly greater compared to that of the QSP formulation, which can be seen in the Table 1. Thus, a scalable xER algorithm can be useful to produce optimal outputs in lesser time. Moreover, with xER, the outputs and the explanations are supported by mathematical guarantees.

Datasets	Nodes	F1		
		xER	F-MWSP	HC
patent_sample	2379	92.0	**94.8**	92.2
csv_example	3337	**95.1**	**95.1**	94.4
settlements	3054	**95.7**	94.4	95.3

Table 4: Dedupe F1 scores

In addition to the F1 scores, other metrics have also been used to evaluate and compare the algorithms' performance. The dataset *settlements* is considered to analyze the algorithms in terms of all the evaluation metrics and is shown in Table 5.

Metric	xER	F-MWSP	HC
F1	**95.7**%	94.4%	95.3 %
Homogeneity	99.8%	99.8 %	**99.9**%
Completeness	**98.9** %	98.5 %	98.7%
V measure	**99.4** %	99.1 %	99.3 %
Adjusted Rand Index	**0.957**	0.944	0.953
Fowlkes Mallows	**0.958**	0.945	0.953

Table 5: Evaluation metrics for *settlements* dataset

6.1.1 Performance of xER on ECB+ Datasets

As discussed in Section 5, smaller datasets are constructed from the ECB+ dataset by performing topic wise modelling from (Barhom et al., 2019). Moreover, instead of performing entity resolution on the whole corpus, a subset of documents from the topics is considered as the input. Smaller datasets of different sizes are generated this way and are used to test and assess the xER algorithm.

After the similarity scores are computed, blocking techniques are applied based on a threshold of T on the similarity scores, in contrast to the blocking before the similarity score generation technique in the benchmarking datasets. The number of edges and the tightness among the nodes, measured by the Clustering Coefficient (CC) (Wang et al., 2017), is varied by varying this threshold T. The xER algorithm is also tested with the groundtruth values as weights. These tests are listed below and analyzed.

6.1.2 Tests Based on Thresholds

As described in Section 5.2, the similarity scores are generated from the normal distribution with means 0.5 and -0.5 depending on the ground truth, and the threshold values belong to the range $[-0.7, -0.2]$. As the threshold T increases, the graph's size becomes smaller due to the removal of edges with a weight less than the T. To demonstrate the impact of thresholding, a graph of 49 nodes is considered, and different graphs are generated from it by applying varying T values and the results are presented in Table 6.

T	|E|	CC	|C|	|MC|	F1	Time (s)		Total Time(s)	
						Phase 1	Phase 2	xER	SPP
-0.7	863	0.739	-	6425	97.33	0.199	9202.66	9202.86	-
-0.5	598	0.512	16619	827	97.33	0.017	4.772	4.780	99.88
-0.3	309	0.315	2906	174	97.33	0.0027	0.465	0.468	31.71
-0.2	228	0.312	2491	108	97.33	0.0017	0.294	0.296	30.2

Table 6: F1 for varying T on a graph of 49 nodes

The graph is denser and tightly connected with a tight threshold. The number of edges (|E|), the clustering coefficient (CC), the number of maximal cliques (|MC|) and the number of all the cliques in the graph (|C|) decrease with increasing T. For a particular T, the input size of SPP (|C|) compared to the input size of QSP (|MC|) is almost exponential and only increases with the graph's size. This difference is reflected in the solution times and can be seen that the SPP solution time is quite large when compared to the xER solution time. With larger graphs, the formulations will be unable to handle this large SPP input size. For the largest graph with $T = -0.7$, the computation time exceeded the time limit and was terminated. Another observation is that tighter thresholds lead to higher computation times for both phase 1 and phase 2. Thus, a higher T value is preferred in terms of solution time and memory management. However, it is possible that blocking with a higher threshold value might lead to a reduction in the recall and affect the F1 scores. So, a moderate threshold is preferred to balance both the F1 scores and the memory issues. T is treated as a hyperparameter, and the optimal T value can be chosen so that the graph size is small enough to handle, and the F1 scores are acceptable. When testing with ground truth values as weights, all the above graphs resulted in a 100% F1 score.

6.1.3 Evaluation: F1 scores

In addition to the thresholding tests, the xER algorithm is tested on other graphs generated using the same approach described above. The threshold value T is set to -0.3. The F1 scores for these graphs are reported in Table 7. As mentioned previously, xER is also tested using the groundtruth values as weights on the edges. xER results in a 100% F1 score when using the groundtruth, in all these datasets, which is also shown in Table 7. This implies that with the best possible scores (groundtruth), the algorithm works perfectly, which highlights the significance of high-quality similarity scores. M is set to 3 for all these graphs, and when the groundtruth is being used as weights, the value of $M = 10$.

This is because the input graph is fully connected because of no thresholding. So Phase 1 returns the whole graph as the maximal clique and phase 2 is responsible for partitiong the whole graph into smaller cliques, which is done using the M value. So a larger value of M enabled the graph to be partitioned into smaller sets as per the weights.

Nodes	Edges	F1-GT (%)	F1 (%)
46	317	100	97.43
135	2589	100	96.46
226	7727	100	91.62
262	10804	100	91.03

Table 7: F1 scores of graphs from the ECB+ dataset.

6.2 Explainability of xER

We now understand the model's explainable nature in an intuitive way with an example. The dataset with 49 nodes and $T = -0.3$ in Table 6 is considered. Three nodes: (7, 12, 20) that form a 3-clique or a triangle in the groundtruth are picked and analyzed. When xER is executed with weights, the thresholding does not remove one node: 25, that is connected to all these three nodes, thus having the potential to form a 4-clique. However, from the Table 8, the total weight that node 25 brings into the triangle is negative (-3.0) and thus, this 4-clique is not a good choice to be included in the optimal solution. Thus, the model automatically prevents this node from forming a 4-clique with the three nodes, thus ensuring that the precision wouldn't decrease. Another important observation is that blocking with a threshold of $T = -0.2$ would have removed the edge between the nodes 20 and 25, thus totally eliminating the potential of forming a 4-clique.

Node 1	Node 2	Weight	Node 1	Node 2	Weight
7	12	0.456	7	25	-0.076
7	20	0.999	12	25	-0.156
12	20	0.085	20	25	-0.253

Table 8: Weights on the edges of nodes (7, 12, 20, 25)

Another example of explainable ER and the importance of having high-quality scores, is considered for the same graph. Four edges: (3-15), (19-29), (21-25), (23-40) with weights $0.316, 0.095, 0.232, 0.046$, respectively, were included in the optimal solution, while these nodes are not connected in the ground truth. The "noisy" weights between these nodes which should have been negative per the ground truth. This shows that a poor scoring scheme can lead to a low quality solution.

As explained in Danilevsky et al. (2020), the explainability of a model can be evaluated in three ways: *Comparison with the groundtruth, Informal explanations and Human evaluation.* We compared the model with ground truth values and obtained the F1 scores. In addition to it, we also performed experiments with the groundtruth scores and the similarity scores to argue the reasoning behind a particular solution. For evaluation through informal explanation, we considered examples from graphs and understood the reasoning behind this output produced by the model. For future work, we plan to include a viable human evaluation technique for the ER problem.

In this paper, we compared our model to an existing approach for ER from Lokhande et al. (2020). As future direction of research, we aim to develop a scalable approach to handle large datasets that would not depend on an off-the-shelf solver to obtain optimal and explainable solutions(with mathematical guarantee), enabling us to compare the performance of xER with more approaches that have been used for ER.

7 Conclusion

A graph partitioning based approach is proposed to solve the entity resolution problem and is formulated as a clique partitioning problem. A node in the graph represents each mention, and the objective was to assign nodes to cliques optimally, and each clique represents a real-world entity. This mathematical formulation based model is inherently explainable. Since CPP is NP-Hard, a two-phased algorithm called xER is proposed and tested on multiple datasets. Phase 1 of xER finds all the graph's maximal cliques, which is much more practical than finding all the cliques in the graph. Phase 2 is a generalized set packing formulation and has a much smaller input size than the traditional set packing problem. These contributions help develop a practical and easily parallelizable implementation for xER. xER shows promising performance in terms of accuracy.

A GPU accelerated approach for xER is in progress and will provide a scalable and practical model. Also, xER can be extended to other applications such as Topic modelling, Community Detection, Temporal Analysis. We believe this paper will lead the way to more mathematical formulation-based approaches and NLP problems can be solved using such highly explainable models, thus reducing the dependency on black-box models.

Acknowledgements

This work is supported by the IBM-ILLINOIS Center for Cognitive Computing Systems Research (C3SR) - a research collaboration as a part of the IBM AI Horizons Network.

References

E. A. Akkoyunlu. 1973. The Enumeration of Maximal Cliques of Large Graphs. SIAM J. Comput., 2(1):1–6.

Mohammad Almasri, Izzat El Hajj, Rakesh Nagi, Jinjun Xiong, and Wen mei Hwu. 2021. Accelerating K-Clique Counting on GPUs. In Proceedings of the 547th International Conference on Very Large Data Bases (VLDB), page submitted.

Vijay Arya, Rachel K. E. Bellamy, Pin-Yu Chen, Amit Dhurandhar, Michael Hind, Samuel C. Hoffman, Stephanie Houde, Q. Vera Liao, Ronny Luss, Aleksandra Mojsilović, Sami Mourad, Pablo Pedemonte, Ramya Raghavendra, John Richards, Prasanna Sattigeri, Karthikeyan Shanmugam, Moninder Singh, Kush R. Varshney, Dennis Wei, and Yunfeng Zhang. 2019. One Explanation Does Not Fit All: A Toolkit and Taxonomy of AI Explainability Techniques. arXiv:1909.03012 [cs, stat]. ArXiv: 1909.03012.

Javed A. Aslam, Ekaterina Pelekhov, and Daniela Rus. 2004. The Star Clustering Algorithm for Static and Dynamic Information Organization. JGAA, 8(1):95–129.

David Aumüller and Erhard Rahm. 2009. Web-based affiliation matching. pages 246–256.

Nikhil Bansal, Avrim Blum, and Shuchi Chawla. 2004. Correlation Clustering. Machine Learning, 56(1-3):89–113.

Shany Barhom, Vered Shwartz, Alon Eirew, Michael Bugert, Nils Reimers, and Ido Dagan. 2019. Revisiting joint modeling of cross-document entity and event coreference resolution. In Proceedings of the 57th Annual Meeting of the Association for Computational Linguistics, pages 4179–4189, Florence, Italy. Association for Computational Linguistics.

Cosmin Bejan and Sanda Harabagiu. 2010. Unsupervised event coreference resolution with rich linguistic features. In Proceedings of the 48th Annual Meeting of the Association for Computational Linguistics, pages 1412–1422, Uppsala, Sweden. Association for Computational Linguistics.

Indrajit Bhattacharya and Lise Getoor. 2004. Iterative record linkage for cleaning and integration. In Proceedings of the 9th ACM SIGMOD workshop on Research issues in data mining and knowledge discovery - DMKD '04, page 11, Paris, France. ACM Press.

Coen Bron and Joep Kerbosch. 1973. Algorithm 457: finding all cliques of an undirected graph. Commun. ACM, 16(9):575–577.

Zheng Chen and Heng Ji. 2009. Graph-based event coreference resolution. In Proceedings of the 2009 Workshop on Graph-based Methods for Natural Language Processing - TextGraphs-4, page 54, Suntec, Singapore. Association for Computational Linguistics.

Zheng Chen and Heng Ji. 2010. Graph-based clustering for computational linguistics: A survey. 2010 Workshop on Graph-based Methods for Natural Language Processing, (July):1–9.

Pramit Choudhary, Aaron Kramer, and datascience.com team. 2018. datascienceinc/Skater: Enable Interpretability via Rule Extraction(BRL).

Agata Cybulska and Piek Vossen. 2014. Using a sledgehammer to crack a nut? lexical diversity and event coreference resolution. In Proceedings of the Ninth International Conference on Language Resources and Evaluation (LREC'14), pages 4545–4552, Reykjavik, Iceland. European Language Resources Association (ELRA).

Marina Danilevsky, Kun Qian, Ranit Aharonov, Yannis Katsis, Ban Kawas, and Prithviraj Sen. 2020. A Survey of the State of Explainable AI for Natural Language Processing. arXiv:2010.00711 [cs]. ArXiv: 2010.00711.

Xavier Delorme, Xavier Gandibleux, and Joaquin Rodriguez. 2004. GRASP for set packing problems. European Journal of Operational Research, 153(3):564–580.

Amr Ebaid, Saravanan Thirumuruganathan, Walid G. Aref, Ahmed Elmagarmid, and Mourad Ouzzani. 2019. Explainer: Entity resolution explanations. In 2019 IEEE 35th International Conference on Data Engineering (ICDE), pages 2000–2003.

Jenny Rose Finkel, Trond Grenager, and Christopher Manning. 2005. Incorporating non-local information into information extraction systems by Gibbs sampling. In Proceedings of the 43rd Annual Meeting on Association for Computational Linguistics - ACL '05, pages 363–370, Ann Arbor, Michigan. Association for Computational Linguistics.

Xavier Gandibleux, Xavier Delorme, and Vincent T'Kindt. 2004. An Ant Colony Optimisation Algorithm for the Set Packing Problem. In David Hutchison, Takeo Kanade, Josef Kittler, Jon M. Kleinberg, Friedemann Mattern, John C. Mitchell, Moni Naor, Oscar Nierstrasz, C. Pandu Rangan, Bernhard Steffen, Madhu Sudan, Demetri Terzopoulos, Dough Tygar, Moshe Y. Vardi, Gerhard Weikum, Marco Dorigo, Mauro Birattari, Christian Blum, Luca Maria Gambardella, Francesco Mondada, and Thomas Stützle, editors, Ant Colony Optimization and Swarm Intelligence, volume 3172, pages 49–60. Springer Berlin Heidelberg, Berlin, Heidelberg. Series Title: Lecture Notes in Computer Science.

Michael R. Garey and David S. Johnson. 2009. Computers and intractability: a guide to the theory of NP-completeness, 27. print edition. A series of books in the mathematical sciences. Freeman, New York [u.a]. OCLC: 551912424.

Forest Gregg and Derek Eder. 2019. Dedupe.

M. Grötschel and Y. Wakabayashi. 1989. A cutting plane algorithm for a clustering problem. Mathematical Programming, 45(1-3):59–96.

Riccardo Guidotti, Anna Monreale, Salvatore Ruggieri, Franco Turini, Fosca Giannotti, and Dino Pedreschi. 2019. A Survey of Methods for Explaining Black Box Models. ACM Computing Surveys, 51(5):1–42.

LLC Gurobi Optimization. 2021. Gurobi optimizer reference manual.

Trevor Hastie, Robert Tibshirani, and Jerome Friedman. 2009. The Elements of Statistical Learning. Springer Series in Statistics. Springer New York, New York, NY.

Manfred Klenner and Étienne Ailloud. 2009. Optimization in coreference resolution is not needed: A nearly-optimal algorithm with intensional constraints. In Proceedings of the 12th Conference of the European Chapter of the Association for Computational Linguistics, EACL '09, page 442–450, USA. Association for Computational Linguistics.

Alexander A. Kolokolov and Lidia A. Zaozerskaya. 2009. On Average Number of Iterations of Some Algorithms for Solving the Set Packing Problem. IFAC Proceedings Volumes, 42(4):1510–1513.

Roy H. Kwon, Georgios V. Dalakouras, and Cheng Wang. 2008. On a posterior evaluation of a simple greedy method for set packing. Optim Lett, 2(4):587–597.

Mercedes Landete, Juan Francisco Monge, and Antonio M. Rodríguez-Chía. 2013. Alternative formulations for the Set Packing Problem and their application to the Winner Determination Problem. Ann Oper Res, 207(1):137–160.

Benjamin Letham, Cynthia Rudin, Tyler H. McCormick, and David Madigan. 2015. Interpretable classifiers using rules and bayesian analysis: Building a better stroke prediction model. The Annals of Applied Statistics, 9(3).

Ruizhi Li, Yupan Wang, Shuli Hu, Jianhua Jiang, Dantong Ouyang, and Minghao Yin. 2020. Solving the Set Packing Problem via a Maximum Weighted Independent Set Heuristic. Mathematical Problems in Engineering, 2020:1–11.

Vishnu Suresh Lokhande, Shaofei Wang, Maneesh Singh, and Julian Yarkony. 2020. Accelerating Column Generation via Flexible Dual Optimal Inequalities with Application to Entity Resolution. arXiv:1909.05460 [cs]. ArXiv: 1909.05460.

Cristina Nicolae and Gabriel Nicolae. 2006. BestCut: a graph algorithm for coreference resolution. In Proceedings of the 2006 Conference on Empirical Methods in Natural Language Processing - EMNLP '06, page 275, Sydney, Australia. Association for Computational Linguistics.

Marco Tulio Ribeiro, Sameer Singh, and Carlos Guestrin. 2016. "why should i trust you?": Explaining the predictions of any classifier. KDD '16, page 1135–1144, New York, NY, USA. Association for Computing Machinery.

Marco Tulio Ribeiro, Sameer Singh, and Carlos Guestrin. 2018. Anchors: High-precision model-agnostic explanations. In AAAI Conference on Artificial Intelligence (AAAI).

Fabrizio Rossi and Stefano Smriglio. 2001. A set packing model for the ground holding problem in congested networks. European Journal of Operational Research, 131(2):400–416.

Mikael Rönnqvist. 1995. A method for the cutting stock problem with different qualities. European Journal of Operational Research, 83(1):57–68.

Alieh Saeedi, Eric Peukert, and Erhard Rahm. 2017. Comparative Evaluation of Distributed Clustering Schemes for Multi-source Entity Resolution. In Mārīte Kirikova, Kjetil Nørvåg, and George A. Papadopoulos, editors, Advances in Databases and Information Systems, volume 10509, pages 278–293. Springer International Publishing, Cham. Series Title: Lecture Notes in Computer Science.

Gregory Tauer, Ketan Date, Rakesh Nagi, and Moises Sudit. 2019. An incremental graph-partitioning algorithm for entity resolution. Information Fusion, 46:171–183.

Ulrike von Luxburg. 2007. A Tutorial on Spectral Clustering. arXiv:0711.0189 [cs]. ArXiv: 0711.0189.

Yu Wang, Eshwar Ghumare, Rik Vandenberghe, and Patrick Dupont. 2017. Comparison of Different Generalizations of Clustering Coefficient and Local Efficiency for Weighted Undirected Graphs. Neural Computation, 29(2):313–331.

Gender Bias in Natural Language Processing Across Human Languages

Abigail Matthews
University of Wisconsin-Madison

Isabella Grasso
Christopher Mahoney
Yan Chen
Esma Wali
Thomas Middleton
Jeanna Matthews
Clarkson University
jnm@clarkson.edu

Mariama Njie
Iona College

Abstract

Natural Language Processing (NLP) systems are at the heart of many critical automated decision-making systems making crucial recommendations about our future world. Gender bias in NLP has been well studied in English, but has been less studied in other languages. In this paper, a team including speakers of 9 languages - Chinese, Spanish, English, Arabic, German, French, Farsi, Urdu, and Wolof - reports and analyzes measurements of gender bias in the Wikipedia corpora for these 9 languages. We develop extensions to profession-level and corpus-level gender bias metric calculations originally designed for English and apply them to 8 other languages, including languages that have grammatically gendered nouns including different feminine, masculine, and neuter profession words. We discuss future work that would benefit immensely from a computational linguistics perspective.

1. Introduction

Corpora of human language are regularly fed into machine learning systems as a key way to learn about the world. Natural Language Processing plays a significant role in many powerful applications such as speech recognition, text translation, and autocomplete and is at the heart of many critical automated decision systems making crucial recommendations about our future world (Yordanov 2018)(Banerjee 2020)(Garbade 2018). Systems are taught to identify spam email, suggest medical articles or diagnoses related to a patient's symptoms, sort resumes based on relevance for a given position, and many other tasks that form key components of critical decision making systems in areas such as criminal justice, credit, housing, allocation of public resources and more.

In a highly influential paper "Man is to Computer Programmer as Woman is to Homemaker? Debiasing Word Embeddings", Bolukbasi et al. (2016) developed a way to measure gender bias using word embedding systems like Word2vec. Specifically, they defined a set of gendered word pairs such as ("he","she") and used the difference between these word pairs to define a gendered vector space. They then evaluated the relationship of profession words like doctor, nurse, or teacher relative to this gendered vector space. They demonstrated that word embedding software trained on a corpus of Google news could associate men with the profession computer programmer and women with the profession homemaker. Systems based on such models, trained even with "representative text" like Google news, could lead to biased hiring practices if used to, for example, parse resumes and suggest matches for a computer programming job. However, as with many results in NLP research, this influential result has not been applied beyond English.

In some earlier work from this team, "Quantifying Gender Bias in Different Corpora", we applied Bolukbasi et al.'s methodology to computing and comparing corpus-level gender bias metrics across different corpora of the English text (Babaeianjelodar 2020). We measured the gender bias in pre-trained models based on a "representative" Wikipedia and Book Corpus in English and compared it to models that had been fine-tuned with various smaller corpora including the General Language Understanding Evaluation (GLUE) benchmarks and two collections of toxic speech, RtGender and IdentityToxic. We found that, as might be expected, the RtGender corpora produced the highest gender bias score. However, we also found that the hate speech corpus, IdentityToxic, had lower gender bias scores than some of more representative corpora found in the GLUE benchmarks. By examining the contents of the IdentityToxic corpus, we found that most of the text in Identity Toxic reflected bias towards race or sexual orientation, rather than gender. These results confirmed the use of a corpus-level gender bias metric as a way of measuring gender bias in an unknown corpus and comparing across corpora, but again was only applied in English.

Here we build on the work of Bolukbasi et al. and our own earlier work to extend these important techniques in gender bias measurement and analysis beyond English. This is challenging because unlike English, many languages like Spanish, Arabic, German, French, and Urdu, have grammatically gendered nouns including feminine, masculine and, neuter or neutral profession words. We translate and modify Bolukbasi et al.'s defining sets and profession sets in English for 8 additional languages and develop exten-

Proceedings of the First Workshop on Trustworthy Natural Language Processing, pages 45–54
June 10, 2021.

sions to the profession-level and corpus-level gender bias metric calculations for languages with grammatically gendered nouns. We use this methodology to analyze the gender bias in Wikipedia corpora for Chinese (Mandarin Chinese), Spanish, English, Arabic, German, French, Farsi, Urdu, and Wolof. We demonstrate how the modern NLP pipeline not only reflects gender bias, but also leads to substantially over-representing some (especially English voices recorded in the digital text) and under-representing most others (speakers of most of the 7000 human languages and even writers of classic works that have not been digitized).

In Section 2, we describe modifications that we made to the defining set and profession set proposed by Bolukbasi et al. in order to extend the methodology beyond English. In Section 3, we discuss the Wikipedia corpora and the occurrence of words in the modified defining and profession sets for 9 languages in Wikipedia. In Section 4, we extend Bolukbasi's gender bias calculation to languages, like Spanish, Arabic, German, French, and Urdu, with grammatically gendered nouns. We apply this to calculate and compare profession-level and corpus-level gender bias metrics for Wikipedia corpora in the 9 languages. We conclude and discuss future work in Section 5. Throughout this paper, we discuss future work that would benefit immensely from a computational linguistics perspective.

2. Modifying Defining Sets and Profession Sets

Word embedding is a powerful NLP technique that represents words in the form of numeric vectors. It is used for semantic parsing, representing the relationship between words, and capturing the context of a word in a document (Karani 2018). For example, Word2vec is a system used to efficiently create word embeddings by using a two-layer neural network that efficiently processes huge data sets with billions of words, and with millions of words in the vocabulary (Mikolov 2013).

Bolukbasi et al. developed a method for measuring gender bias using word embedding systems like Word2vec. Specifically, they defined a set of highly gendered word pairs such as ("he", "she") and used the difference between these word pairs to define a gendered vector space. They then evaluated the relationship of profession words like doctor, nurse or teacher relative to this gendered vector space. Ideally, profession words would not reflect a strong gender bias. However, in practice, they often do. According to such a metric, doctor might be male biased or nurse female biased based on how these words are used in the corpora from which the word embedding model was produced. Thus, this gender bias metric of profession words as calculated from the Word2Vec model can be used as a measure of the gender bias learned from corpora of natural language.

In this section, we describe the modifications we made to the defining set and profession set proposed by Bolukbasi et al. in order to extend the methodology beyond English. Before applying these changes to other languages, we evaluate the impact of the changes on calculations in English. In this section, we also describe the Wikipedia corpora we used across 9 languages and analyze the occurrences of our defining set and profession set words in these corpora. This work is also described, but with a different focus in Wali et al. (2020) and Chen et al. (2021).

2.1. Defining Set

The defining set is a list of gendered word pairs used to define what a gendered relationship looks like. Bolukbasi et al's original defining set contained 10 English word pairs (she-he, daughter-son, her-his, mother-father, woman-man, gal-guy, Mary-John, girl-boy, herself-himself, and female-male) (Bobluski et al. 2016). We began with this set, but made substantial changes in order to compute gender bias effectively across 9 languages.

Specifically, we removed 6 of the 10 pairs, added 3 new pairs and translated the final set into 8 additional languages. For example, we removed the pairs she-he and herself-himself because they are the same word in some languages like Wolof, Farsi, Urdu, and German. Similarly, we removed the pair her-his because in some languages like French and Spanish, the gender of the object does not depend on the person to which it belongs.

We also added 3 new pairs (queen-king, wife-husband, and madam-sir) for which more consistent translations were available across languages. Interestingly, as we will discuss, the pair wife-husband introduces surprising results in many languages. Our final defining set for this study thus contained 7 word pairs and Table 1 shows our translations of this final defining set across the 9 languages included in our study.

2.2 Professions Set

We began with Bolukbasi et al's profession word set in English, but again made substantial changes in order to compute gender bias effectively across 9 languages. Bolukbasi et al. had an original list of 327 profession words (2016), including some words that would not technically be classified as professions like saint or drug addict. We narrowed this list down to 32 words including: nurse, teacher, writer, engineer, scientist, manager, driver, banker, musician, artist, chef, filmmaker, judge, comedian, inventor, worker, soldier, journalist, student, athlete, actor, governor, farmer, person, lawyer, adventurer, aide, ambassador, analyst, astronaut, astronomer, and biologist. We tried to choose a diverse set of professions from creative to scientific, from high-paying to lower-paying, etc. that occured in as many of the 9 languages as we could. As with Bolukbasi et al.'s profession set, one of our profession words, person, is not technically a profession, but we kept it because, unlike many professions, it is especially likely

English	Chinese	Spanish	Arabic	German	French	Farsi	Urdu	Wolof
woman	女人	mujer	النساء	Frau	femme	زن	عورت	Jigéen
man	男人	hombre	رجل	Mann	homme	مرد	آدمی	Góor
daughter	女儿	hija	ابنة	Tochter	fille	دختر	بیٹی	Doom ju jigéen
son	儿子	hijo	ولد	Sohn	fils	پسر	بیٹا	Doom ju góor
mother	母亲	madre	ام	Mutter	mère	مادر	ماں	Yaay
father	父亲	padre	اب	Vater	père	پدر	باپ	Baay
girl	女孩	niña	ابنة	Mädchen	fille	دختر	لڑکی	Janxa
boy	男孩	niño	صبي	Junge	garçon	پسر	لڑکا	Xale bu góor
queen	女王	reina	ملكة	Königin	reine	ملکہ	ملکہ	Jabari buur
king	国王	rey	ملك	König	roi	پادشاه	بادشاہ	Buur
wife	妻子	esposa	زوجة	Ehefrau	épouse	همسر	بیوی	Jabar
husband	丈夫	esposo	الزوج	Ehemann	mari	شوهر	شوہر	jëkkër
madam	女士	señora	سيدتي	Dame	madame	خانم	محترمہ	Ndawsi
sir	男士	señor	سيدي	Herr	monsieur	آقا	جناب	Góorgui

Table 1: Final defining set translated across languages. Note: Wolof is primarily a spoken language and is often written as it would be pronounced in English, French and Arabic. This table shows it written as it would be pronounced in French.

to have a native word in most human languages.

The primary motivation for reducing the profession set from 327 to 32 was to reduce the work needed to translate and validate all of them in 9 languages. Even with 32 words, there were substantial complexities in translation. As we mentioned, languages with grammatically gendered nouns can have feminine, masculine, and neuter words for the same profession. For instance, in Spanish, the profession "writer" will be translated as "escritora" for women and "escritor" for men, but the word for journalist, "periodista", is used for both women and men.

Profession words are often borrowed from other languages. In this study, we found that Urdu and Wolof speakers often use the English word for a profession when speaking in Urdu or Wolof. In some cases, there is a word for that profession in the language as well and in some cases, there is not. For example, in Urdu, it is more common to use the English word "manager" when speaking even though there are Urdu words for the profession manager. In written Urdu, manager could be written directly in English characters (manager) or written phonetically as the representation of the word manager using Urdu/Arabic characters (مینجر) or written as an Urdu word for manager (منتظم /منتظمہ).

A similar pattern occurs in Wolof and also in Wolof there are some additional complicating factors. Wolof is primarily a spoken language that when written is transcribed phonetically. This may be done using English, French, or Arabic character sets and pronunciation rules. Thus, for the same pronunciation, spelling can vary substantially and this complicates NLP processing such as with Word2Vec significantly. After making these substantial changes to the defining sets and profession sets, the first thing we did was analyze their impact on gender bias measurements in English. Using both Bolukbasi et al's original defining and professions sets and our modified sets, we computed the gender bias scores on the English Wikipedia corpus. With our 7 defining set pairs and 32 profession words, we conducted a T-test and even with these substantial changes the T-test results were insignificant, inferring that the resulting gender bias scores in both instances have no statistically significant difference for the English Wikipedia corpus. This result was an encouraging validation that our method was measuring the same effects as in Bolukbasi et al. even with the modified and reduced defining set and profession set.

While our goal in this study was to identify a defining set and profession set that could more easily be used across many languages and for which the T-test results indicated no statistically significant difference in results over the English Wikipedia corpus, it would be interesting to repeat this analysis with additional variations in the defining set and profession set. For example, we considered adding additional pairs like sister-brother or grandmother-grandfather. In some languages like Chinese, Arabic, and Wolof, there are different words for younger and older sister or brother. We also considered and discarded many other profession words such as bartender, policeman, celebrity, and electrician. For example, we discarded bartender because it is not a legal profession in some countries. We would welcome collaborators from the computational linguistics community to help identify promising defining set pairs and profession set words which which to experiment.

3. Wikipedia Corpora Across Languages

Bolukbasi et al. applied their gender bias calculations to a Word2Vec model trained with a corpus of Google news in English. In Babaeianjelodar et al., we used the same defining and profession sets as Bolukbasi et al. to compute gender bias metrics for a BERT model trained with Wikipedia and a BookCorpus also in English. In this paper, we train Word2Vec models using our modified defining and profession sets and the Wikipedia corpora for 9 languages. Specifically, we use the Chinese, Spanish, Arabic, German, French, Farsi, Urdu, and Wolof corpora downloaded from Wikipedia on 2020-06-20. We would like to examine more languages in this way and would welcome suggestions of languages to prioritize in future work.

3.1. Differences in Wikipedia across Languages

While there are Wikipedia corpora for all 9 of our languages, they differ substantially in size and quality. Wikipedia is a very commonly used dataset for testing NLP tools and even for building pre-trained models. However, for many reasons, a checkmark simply saying that a Wikipedia corpus exists for a language hides many caveats to full representation and participation. In addition to variation in size and quality across languages, not all speakers of a language have equal access to contributing to Wikipedia. For example, in the case of Chinese, Chinese speakers in mainland China have little access to Wikipedia because it is banned by the Chinese government (Siegel 2019). Thus, Chinese articles in Wikipedia are more likely to have been contributed by the 40 million Chinese speakers in Taiwan, Hong Kong, Singapore, and elsewhere (Su 2019). In other cases, the percentage of speakers with access to Wikipedia may vary for other reasons such as access to computing devices and Internet access.

Using Wikipedia as the basis of pre-trained models and testing of NLP tools also means that the voices of those producing digital text are prioritized. Even authors of classic works of literature that fundamentally shaped cultures are under-represented in favor of writers typing Wikipedia articles on their computer or even translating text written in other languages with automated tools.

3.2. Word Count Results

One critical aspect of our process was to examine the number of times each word in our defining set (7 pairs) and 32 profession words occurs in the Wikipedia corpus for each language. This proved an invaluable step in refining our defining and profession sets, understanding the nature of the Wikipedia corpora themselves, catching additional instances where NLP tools were not designed to handle the complexities of some languages, and even catching simple errors in our own translations and process. For example, when our original word count results for German showed a count of zero for all words, we discovered that even though all nouns in German are capitalized, in the Word2vec processed Wikipedia corpus for German, all words were in lowercase. This was an easy problem to fix, but illustrates the kind of "death by a thousand cuts" list of surprising errors that can occur for many languages throughout the NLP pipeline.

One important limitation to note is that for many languages, if a word is expressed with a multi-word phrase (e.g. astronomer(عالِم الفلك) in Arabic), the word count reported by Word2Vec for this phrase will be zero. For each language, there is a tokenizer that identifies the words or phrases to be tracked. In many cases, the tokenizer identifies words as being separated by a space. The Chinese tokenizer however attempts to recognize when multiple characters that are separated with spaces should be tracked as a multi-character word or concept. This involves looking up a string of characters in a dictionary. Once again this demonstrates the types of surprising errors that can occur for many languages throughout the NLP pipeline. It is also possible to add the word vectors for component words together as a measure of the multi-word pair, but this is not always ideal. In this study, we did not attempt this, but it would be interesting future work.

Another important factor is that the Wikipedia corpora for some languages are quite small. In Wolof, for example, only two of our profession words occurred ("nit", the word for person, occurred 1401 times and waykat, the word for musician, occurred 5 times). This is partly because of multi-word pairs and partly because of variants in spelling. However, we think it is especially due to the small size of the Wolof corpus because the percentage of profession words amongst the total words for Wolof is similar to that of other languages. Across the 9 languages, the percentage of profession words varied from 0.014% and 0.037%. Wolof actually had one of the higher percentages at 0.026%. However, its overall Wikipedia corpus is tiny (1422 articles or less than 1% of the number of articles even in Urdu, the next smallest corpora) and that simply isn't a lot of text with which to work. Even so, Wolof is still better represented in Wikipedia than the vast majority of the over 7000 human languages spoken today! This is another clear illustration of how the gap in support for so many languages leads directly to the under-representation of many voices in NLP-guided decision-making.

We do not have room to include the word counts for the defining sets and profession sets for all 9 languages here, but an expanded technical report with this data is available at http://tinyurl.com/clarksonnlpbias.

4. Extending Profession and Corpora Level Gender Bias Metrics

We have already described how we established a modified defining set and profession set for use across 9 languages and then evaluated the use of these sets of words in Wikipedia. We also described how we used the Wikipedia corpora of these 9 languages to train

Word2Vec models for each language. In this section, we describe how we extend Bolukbasi et al.'s method for computing the gender bias of each word.

We begin with Bolukbasi et al.'s method for computing a gender bias metric for each word. Specifically, each word is expressed as a vector by Word2Vec and we calculate the center of the vectors for each definitional pair. For example, to calculate the center of the definitional pair she/he, we average the vector for "she" with the vector for "he". Then, we calculate the distance of each word in the definitional pair from the center by subtracting the center from each word in the pair (e.g. "she" - center). We then apply Principal Component Analysis (PCA) to the matrix of these distances. PCA is an approach that compresses multiple dimensions into fewer dimensions, ideally in a way that the information within the original data is not lost. Usually the number of reduced dimensions is 1-3 as it allows for easier visualization of a dataset. Bolukbasi et al. used the first eigenvalue from the PCA matrix (i.e. the one that is larger than the rest). Because the defining set pairs were chosen to the highly gendered, they expect this dimension to be relate primarily to gender and therefore call it the gender direction or the g direction. (Note: The effectiveness of this compression can vary and in some cases, the first eigenvalue may not actually be much larger than the second. We see cases of this in our study as we will discuss.) Finally, we use Bolukbasi et al.'s formula for direct gender bias:

$$\text{DirectBias}_c = \frac{1}{|N|} \sum_{w \in N} |\cos(\overrightarrow{w}, g)|^c \qquad (1)$$

where N represents the list of profession words, g represents the gender direction calculated, w represents each profession word, and c is a parameter to measure the strictness of the bias. In this paper, we used $c = 1$; c values and their effects are explained in more detail in Bolukbasi et al. We examine this gender bias score both for the individual words as well as an average gender bias across profession words as a measure of gender bias in a corpus.

To apply this methodology across languages, some important modifications and extensions were required, especially to handle languages, like Spanish, Arabic, German, French, and Urdu, that have grammatically gendered nouns. In this section, we describe our modifications and apply them to computing and comparing both profession-level and corpus-level gender bias metrics across the Wikipedia corpora for 9 languages.

4.1. Evaluating the Gender Bias of Defining Sets Across Languages

To begin, in Figure 1, we present the gender bias scores, calculated as described above according to Bolukbasi et al.'s methodology, for each of our 14 defining set words (7 pairs) across 9 languages. Female gender bias is represented as a positive number (red bar) and male gender bias is represented as a negative number (blue bar). Not all defining set words occur in the Wikipedia corpus for Wolof. Some because they are translated in multi-word phrases and some simply because of the same size of the corpora.

The defining set pairs were specifically chosen because we expect them to be highly gendered. In most cases, the defining set words indicated male or female bias as expected, but there were some exceptions. One common exception was the word husband. Husband, somewhat surprisingly, has a female bias in a number of languages. We hypothesize that "husband" may more often be used in relationship to women (e.g. "her husband"). One might guess that the same pattern would happen for wife then but it does not appear to be the case. We hypothesize that it may be less likely for a man to be defined as a husband outside of a female context, where women may often be defined by their role as a wife even when not in the context of the husband. This is an interesting effect we saw across many languages.

In Figure 2, we aggregate the gender bias for all the male words (sir, husband, king, etc.) and all the female words (madam, wife, queen, etc.) This presentation emphasizes several key aspects of the results. For example, we can see that for Spanish, English, Arabic, German, French, Farsi, and Urdu, that the female words are female leaning and that most male words and male leaning as one might expect,with the exception of husband in all of these languages and also man in Farsi. We can also see that female words have more female bias than male words have male bias.

We can also see problems with both Chinese and Wolof. We have discussed some of the problems in Wolof with the size of the corpora and the difficulty of matching phonetically transcribed words. However, for Chinese, we have a sizable corpora and many occurrences of the defining set words. After much investigation, we isolated an issue related to the Principal Component Analysis (PCA) in Chinese. As we described at the beginning of this section, Bolukbasi et al.'s methodology calls for using the largest eigenvalue and in their experience the first eigenvalue was much larger than the second and they analyzed their results using only this dominant dimension. However, we found that this was not always the case. In particular for the Chinese Wikipedia corpus, the largest eigenvalue of the PCA matrix is not much larger than the second.

In Figure 3, we report the difference in PCA scores between the dominant component and the next most dominant component across 9 languages in our study. We also add a bar for the value Bolukbasi et al. reported for the Google News Corpora in English that they analyzed. Chinese has the lowest. Wolof has the highest with 1.0, but only because there were not enough defining pairs to meaningfully perform dimension reduction into 2 dimensions. We repeated our analysis without the wife-husband pair and found that the difference in PCA scores improved for all languages except for

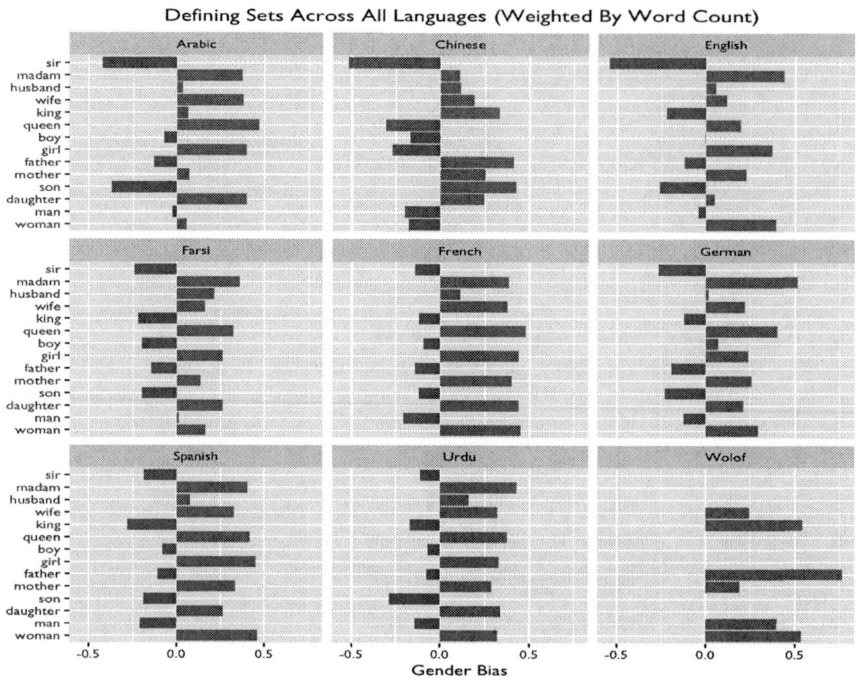

Figure 1: Defining Sets Across Languages The x-axis represents per-word gender bias scores as proposed by Bolukbasi et al. Female gender bias is represented as a positive number (red bar) and male gender bias is represented as a negative number (blue bar). Not all defining set words occur in the small Wikipedia corpus for Wolof. We note that boy in English has a gender bias of -0.002 which is such a small blue line that it is difficult to see.

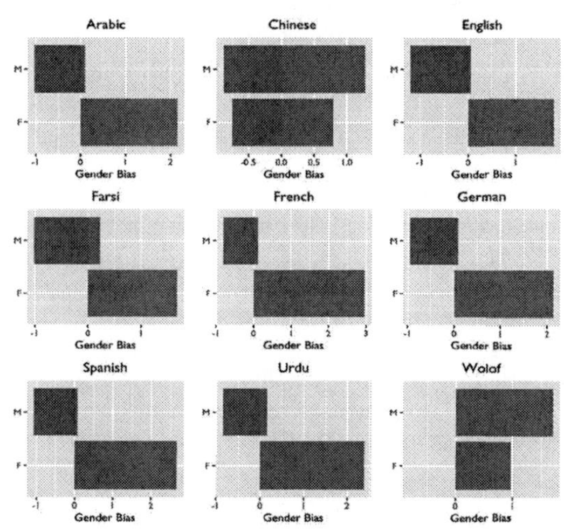

Figure 2: Defining Set Summary For each language, we aggregate the gender bias scores of male defining set words (the M bar) and female defining set words (the F bar).

Wolof. Wolof remains 1.0 because we didn't find any defining pairs. We have been experimenting with modifications to the defining set in Chinese including isolating the contribution of each individual defining set pair and adding many pairs that while meaningful specifi-

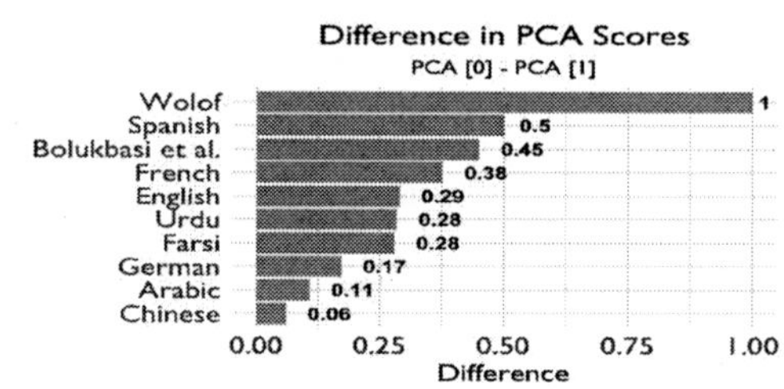

Figure 3: Difference in importance between first and second principal components by language. A larger difference increases the confidence we've isolated the gender direction.

cally in Chinese would not have worked well across all languages (e.g. different pairs for paternal and maternal grandmother and grandfather). However, we have yet to find a defining set that works well and would welcome collaborations from linguists with expertise in Chinese.

The word boy in German, Junge, also highlights some important issues. Junge can also be used as an adjective such as in "junge Leute" (young people) and it is also a common surname. Since these different uses of the word are not disambiguated, it is likely that the token "junge" encompasses more meaning than simply boy. We also saw this with the defining set word "fille" in French which means both girl and daughter. This

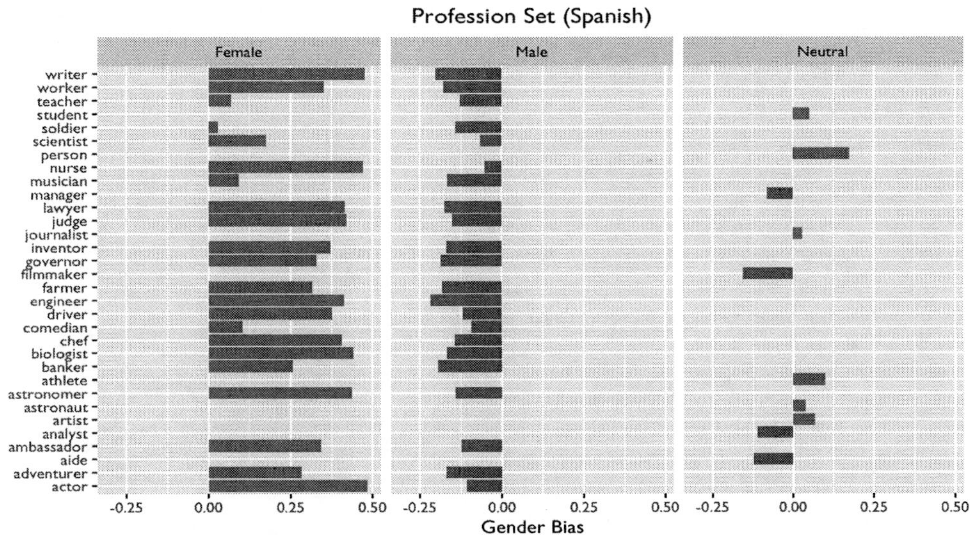

Figure 4: Per Profession Gender Bias for Spanish. Broken down into female only variants, male only variants and neutral variants.

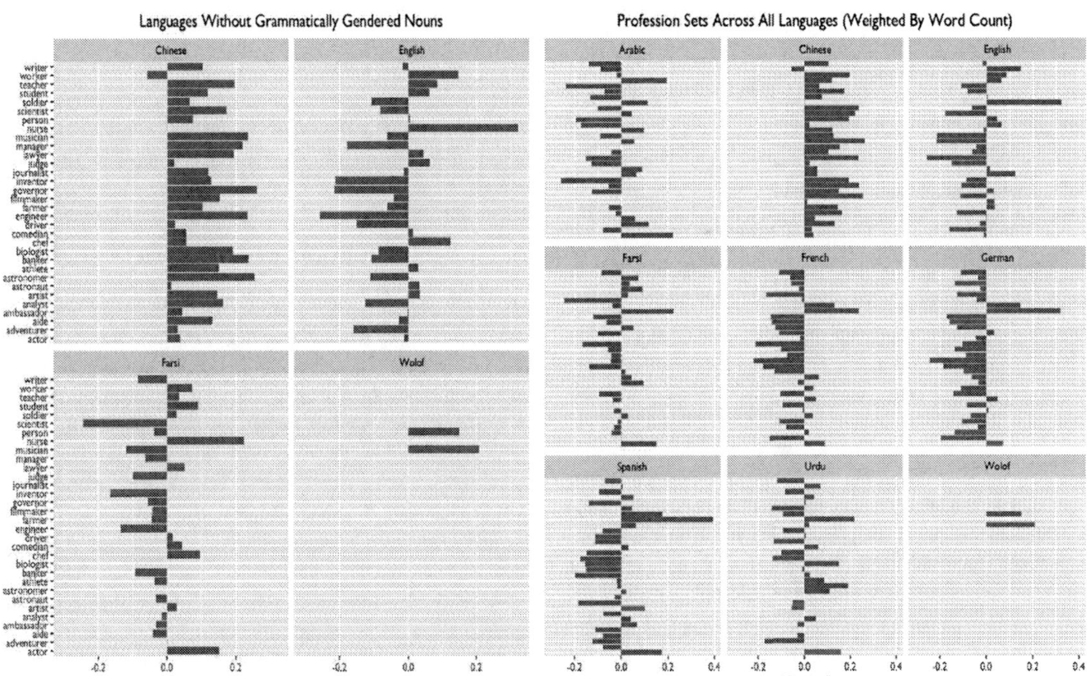

Figure 5: (LEFT)Per-Profession Gender Bias Metrics for Languages Without Grammatically Gendered Nouns (RIGHT)Per-Profession Gender Bias Metrics for All Languages Weighting by Word Count

problem of disambiguation occurs in many languages and multiple meanings for words should be considered when selecting terms. We would appreciate the insight of linguists in how to handle disambiguation of terms more generally.

4.2. Evaluating the Gender Bias of Profession Sets Across Languages

Having analyzed the defining set results where there is a clearly expected gender for each word, we move on to the question of computing the gender bias scores for each of our 32 profession words. Bolukbasi et al.'s methodology can be applied directly in English and also in other languages which, like English, do not have many grammatically gendered nouns. Of the 9 languages, we studied, Chinese, Farsi and Wolof are also in this category.

The situation is more complicated in languages with grammatically gendered nouns. Five of the languages we are studying fall into this category: Spanish, Arabic, German, French, and Urdu. In these languages, many professions have both a feminine and masculine form. In some cases, there is also a neutral form and in some cases there is only a neutral form. In Section 2.2, we discussed how Urdu also often uses English words directly. Thus there are neutral Urdu words and neutral English words used in Urdu. To form a per-profession bias metric, we averaged the bias metrics of these various forms in several different ways. First, we averaged them, weighting each different form of a profession equally. However, we found that this overestimated the female bias in many cases. For example, in German the male form of scientist, Wissenschaftler, has a slight male gender bias (-0.06) and the female form, Wissenschaftlerin, has a strong female gender bias (0.32). When averaged together evenly, we would get an overall female gender bias of 0.13. However, the male form occurs 32,467 times in the German Wikipedia corpus while the female form occurs only 1354 times. To take this difference into account, we computed a weighted average resulting in an overall male gender bias of -0.04. With this weighted average, we could observe intuitive patterns across languages with grammatically gendered nouns and languages without. This increases our confidence in the usefulness of these profession level metrics and in particular the weighted average.

In Figure 4, we show an example breakdown of the gender bias scores for the Spanish profession words. We show female only variants, male only variants and neutral only variants. At http://tinyurl/clarksonnlpbias, we provide a technical report with a breakdown like this for all 5 of the gendered languages in our study. Notice that the gender bias for all female words is indeed female and that the gender bias for all male words is indeed male. Neutral words show a mix of male and female bias. This an intuitive and encouraging result that further supports the use of per-word gender bias calculations across languages. This is often true in other languages, but not exclusively so.

In Figure 5, we compare these profession-level gender bias scores across languages. On the left, we show results for the languages without grammatically gendered nouns. On the right, we show results across all languages using the weighted average (weighted by word count).

In Figure 6, we use Pearson's correlation for cluster analysis to examine 7 languages, omitting Chinese and Wolof because of problems with PCA and corpora size. This exploratory analysis provokes a number of questions for future work including: How do linguistics inform bias outputs (e.g. If English is a mixture of Germanic and Latin languages, is that why it's clustered with those languages even though it's not gendered?) and How does a language being inherently gendered affect the resulting bias of a NLP model in that language?

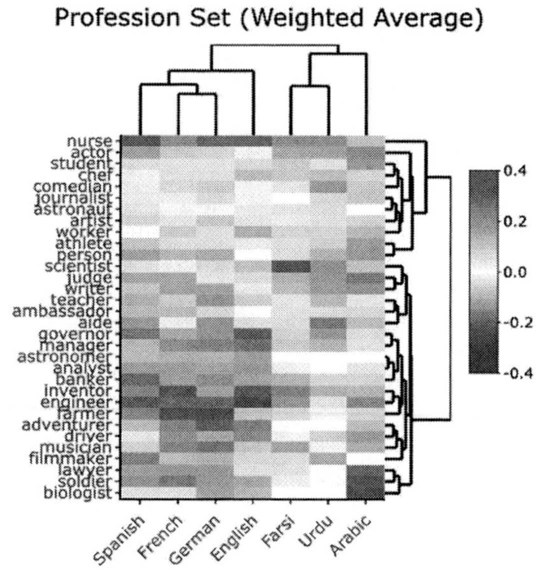

Figure 6: Pearson's correlation for cluster analysis across 7 languages

6. Conclusion and Future Work

We have extended an influential method for computing gender bias from Bolukbasi et al., a technique that had only been applied in English. We made key modifications that allowed us to extend the methodology to 8 additional languages, including languages with grammatically gendered nouns. With this, we quantified how gender bias varies across the Wikipedia corpora of 9 languages and discuss future work that could benefit immensely from a computational linguistics perspective.

Specifically, we would like to explore additional languages as well as understand better how variations in defining sets and profession sets can highlight differences among languages. We would like to compare gender bias across different corpora of culturally important texts written by native speakers. Even within one language, we would like to examine collections with different emphasis such as gender of author, different time periods, different genres of text, different country of origin,etc. Our work is an important first step toward quantifying and comparing gender bias across languages - what we can measure, we can more easily begin to track and improve, but it is only a start. The majority of human languages need more useful tools and resources to overcome the barriers such that we can build NLP tools with less gender bias.

Acknowledgements

We'd like to thank the Clarkson Open Source Institute for their help and support with infrastructure and hosting of our experiments. We'd like to thank Golshan Madraki, Marzieh Babaeianjelodar, and Ewan Middelton for help with language translations as well as our wider team including William Smialek, Graham Northup, Cameron Weinfurt, Joshua Gordon, and Hunter Bashaw for their support.

References

Babaeianjelodar, M.; Lorenz, S.; Gordon, J.; Matthews, J.; and Freitag, E. 2020. Quantifying gender bias in different corpora. In Companion Proceedings of the Web Conference 2020, WWW '20, page 752–759, New York, NY, USA, 2020. Association for Computing Machinery. DOI: https://doi.org/10.1145/3366424.3383559.

Banerjee, D. 2020. Natural Language Processing (NLP) Simplified: A Step-by-step Guide. Datascience foundation. Retrieved from https://datascience.foundation/sciencewhitepaper/natural-language-processing-nlp-simplified-a-step-by-step-guide

BERT. 2020. BERT Pretrained models. Github. Retrieved from https://github.com/google-research/bert#bert

Bolukbasi, T.; Chang, K.; Zou, J. Y.; Saligrama, V.; and Kalai, A.T. 2016. Man is to computer programmer as woman is to homemaker? debiasing word embeddings. In Advances in neural information processing systems, pp. 4349-4357.

Buolamwini, J; and Gebru T. 2018. Gender Shades: Intersectional Accuracy Disparities in Commercial Gender Classification. Proceedings of the 1st Conference on Fairness, Accountability and Transparency, PMLR 81:77-91, 2018.

Bussieck, J. 2017. Demystifying Word2Vec. Retrieved from https://www.deeplearningweekly.com/blog/demystifying-word2vec/

Chen, Y., Mahoney, C., Grasso, I., Wali, E., Matthews, A., Middleton, T., Njie, M., and Matthews, J. Gender Bias and Under-Representation in Natural Language Processing Across Human Languages Proceedings of the 2021 AAAI/ACM Conference on Artificial Intelligence, Ethics and Society (AIES), May 19-21 2021.

Devlin, J., Chang, M. W., Lee, K., & Toutanova, K. 2018. Bert: Pre-training of deep bidirectional transformers for language understanding. arXiv:1810.04805. Retrieved from https://arxiv.org/abs/1810.04805

Devlin, J., Chang, M. W., Lee, K., & Toutanova, K. 2018. Bert: Pre-training of deep bidirectional transformers for language understanding. arXiv:1810.04805. Retrieved from https://arxiv.org/abs/1810.04805

Garbade, M. J. 2018. A Simple Introduction To Natural Language Processing. Retrieved from https://becominghuman.ai/a-simple-introduction-to-natural-language-processing-ea66a1747b32

Holley, R. 2009. How good can it get? Analysing and improving OCR accuracy in large scale historic newspaper digitisation programs. D-Lib Magazine, March/April 2009, Volume 15 Number 3/4 ISSN 1082-9873. Retrieved from http://www.dlib.org/dlib/march09/holley/03holley.html

Karani, D. 2018. Introduction to Word Embedding and Word2Vec. Retrieved from https://towardsdatascience.com/introduction-to-word-embedding-and-word2vec-652d0c2060fa

Karch, M. 2020. How to Use the Ngram Viewer Tool in Google Books. Retrieved from https://www.lifewire.com/google-books-ngram-viewer-1616701

Mikolov, T.; Chen, K.; Corrado, G.; and Dean, J. 2013. Efficient estimation of word representations in vector space. arXiv:1301.3781. Retrieved from https://arxiv.org/abs/1301.3781

Mithe, R.; Indalkar, S.; and Divekar, N. 2013. Optical character recognition. International journal of recent technology and engineering. ISSN: 2277-3878, Volume-2, Issue-1, March 2013.

NLTK. 2005. Natural Language Toolkit. Retrieved from http://www.nltk.org/

Nosek, B. A.; Banaji, M. R.; and Greenwald, A. G. 2002. Harvesting implicit group attitudes and beliefs from a demonstration web site. Group Dynamics: Theory, Research, and Practice, 6(1):101, 2002. Ohio University. Wolof Language. Retrieved from https://www.ohio.edu/cis/african/languages/wolof

Rong, X. 2016. word2vec Parameter Learning Explained. arXiv:1411.2738. Retrieved from https://arxiv.org/abs/1411.2738

Siegel, R. 2019. Search result not found: China bans Wikipedia in all languages. Retrieved from https://www.washingtonpost.com/business/2019/05/15/china-bans-wikipedia-all-languages/

Su, Q, G. 2019. Which Parts of the World Speaks Mandarin Chinese?. Retrieved from https://www.thoughtco.com/where-is-mandarin-spoken-2278443

Wali, E., Chen, Y., Mahoney, C., Middleton, T., Babaeianjelodar, M., Njie, M., and Matthews, J. Is Machine Learning Speaking my Language? A Critical Look at the NLP-Pipeline Across 8 Human Languages Participatory ML Workshop,Thirty-seventh International Conference on Machine Learning (ICML 2020), July 17 2020.

WikipediaA. 2020. Wikipedia: German language. Retrieved from https://en.wikipedia.org/wiki/German_language

WikipediaB. 2020. Wikipedia: List of languages by total number of speakers. Retrieved from https://en.wikipedia.org/wiki/List_of_languages_by_total_number_of_speakers

WikipediaC. 2020. Wikipedia: List of Wikipedias. Retrieved from https://en.wikipedia.org/wiki/List_of_Wikipedias

WikipediaD. 2020. Wikipedia: Wolof Wikipedia. Retrieved from https://en.wikipedia.org/wiki/Wolof_Wikipedia

Williams, A., Nangia, N., Bowma, S. 2020. MultiNLI, The Multi-Genre NLI Corpus. Retrieved from https://cims.nyu.edu/~sbowman/multinli

Yordanov, V. 2018. Introduction To Natural Language Processing For Text. Medium. Retrieved from https://towardsdatascience.com/introduction-to-natural-lan guage-processing-for-text-df845750fb63

Yamada, I.; Asai, A.; Sakuma, J.; Shindo, H.; Takeda, H.; Takefuji, Y.; and Matsumoto Y. 2018. Wikipedia2Vec: An Efficient Toolkit for Learning and Visualizing the Embeddings of Words and Entities from Wikipedia. arXiv:1812.06280. Retrieved from https://arxiv.org/abs/1812.06280

Interpreting Text Classifiers by Learning Context-sensitive Influence of Words

Sawan Kumar*
IISc, Bangalore, India
sawankumar@iisc.ac.in

Kalpit Dixit
Amazon AWS AI, USA
kddixit@amazon.com

Kashif Shah
Amazon AWS AI, USA
shahkas@amazon.com

Abstract

Many existing approaches for interpreting text classification models focus on providing importance scores for parts of the input text, such as words, but without a way to test or improve the interpretation method itself. This has the effect of compounding the problem of understanding or building trust in the model, with the interpretation method itself adding to the opacity of the model. Further, importance scores on individual examples are usually not enough to provide a sufficient picture of model behavior. To address these concerns, we propose MOXIE (MOdeling conteXt-sensitive InfluencE of words) with an aim to enable a richer interface for a user to interact with the model being interpreted and to produce testable predictions. In particular, we aim to make predictions for importance scores, counterfactuals and learned biases with MOXIE. In addition, with a global learning objective, MOXIE provides a clear path for testing and improving itself. We evaluate the reliability and efficiency of MOXIE on the task of sentiment analysis.

Input text: *he played a homosexual character*
Model prediction: Negative sentiment[1]

Question 1 (Importance scores): Which words had the most influence towards the prediction? Is the word '*homosexual*' among them?
Answer: The word '*homosexual*' has the highest negative influence.

Question 2 (Counterfactuals): If so, which words instead would have made the prediction positive?
Answer: If you replace the word '*homosexual*' with the word '*straight*', the model would have made a positive sentiment prediction.

Question 3 (Biases): Is there a general bias against the word '*homosexual*' compared to the word '*straight*'?
Answer: Yes, there are a large number of contexts where the model predicts negatively with the word '*homosexual*', but positively with the word '*straight*'. Here are some examples:

- *the most* ***homosexual*** *thing about this film*
- *though it's equally* ***homosexual*** *in tone*
- ...

Table 1: *Example questions we aim to answer using MOXIE.* The first question has commonly been addressed in existing approaches. The ability of an interpretation method to answer the second and third questions enables a rich and testable interface.

1 Introduction

Interpretability, while under-specified as a goal, is a crucial requirement for artificial intelligence (AI) agents (Lipton, 2018). For text classification models, where much of the recent success has come from large and opaque neural network models (Devlin et al., 2019; Liu et al., 2019; Raffel et al., 2019), a popular approach to enable interpretability is to provide importance scores for parts of the input text, such as words, or phrases. Given only these numbers, it is difficult for a user to understand or build trust in the model. Going beyond individual examples, such as scalable and testable methods to identify biases at a dataset level, are desired but currently missing. Questions can be raised about whether the methods of interpretation themselves are trustworthy. Recent analyses (Ghorbani et al., 2019) of such interpretation methods for computer vision tasks suggest that such skepticism is valid and important.

A method which aims to elucidate a black-box's behavior should not create additional black boxes. Measuring trustworthiness, or faithfulness[2], of interpretation methods, is itself a challenging task (Jacovi and Goldberg, 2020). Human evaluation is not only expensive, but as Jacovi and Goldberg (2020) note human-judgments of quality shouldn't

*Work done during an internship at Amazon AWS AI, USA.

[1]No offense is intended towards any particular community in this or in subsequent sections. Rather, we are interested in probing for unexpected biases.

[2]In this work, a faithful interpretation is one which is aligned with the model's reasoning process. The focus of this work is to make predictions testable by the model being interpreted and thus have a clear measure of faithfulness.

Proceedings of the First Workshop on Trustworthy Natural Language Processing, pages 55–67
June 10, 2021. ©2021 Association for Computational Linguistics

be used to test the faithfulness of importance scores. What needs testing is whether these scores reflect what has been learned by the model being interpreted, and not whether they are plausible scores.

We believe the aforementioned issues in existing methods that produce importance scores can be circumvented through the following changes.

A global learning objective: Several existing approaches rely on some heuristic to come up with importance scores, such as gradients (Wallace et al., 2019), attentions (Wiegreffe and Pinter, 2019), or locally valid classifiers (Ribeiro et al., 2016) (see Atanasova et al. (2020) for a broad survey). Instead, we propose to identify a global learning objective which, when learned, enables prediction of importance scores, with the assumption that if the learning objective was learned perfectly, we would completely trust the predictions. This would provide a clear path for testing and improving the interpretation method itself. Quick and automatic evaluation on a held-out test set allows progress using standard Machine Learning (ML) techniques.

Going beyond importance scores: Importance scores, even when generated using a theoretically inspired framework (Sundararajan et al., 2017), are generally hard to evaluate. Further, the aim of the interpretation method shouldn't be producing importance scores alone, but to enable a user to explore and understand model behavior[3], potentially over large datasets. In Table 1, we illustrate a way to do that through a set of questions that the interpretation method should answer. Here, we provide more details on the same.

Importance Scores 'Which parts of the input text were most influential for the prediction?' Such importance scores, popular in existing approaches, can provide useful insights but are hard to evaluate.

Counterfactuals 'Can it predict counterfactuals?' We define a good counterfactual as one with minimal changes to the input text while causing the model to change its decision. Such predictions can be revealing but easy to test. They can provide insights into model behavior across a potentially large vocabulary of words.

In this work, we consider counterfactuals obtained by replacing words in the input text with other words in the vocabulary. We limit to one replacement.

Biases 'Is the model biased against certain words?' For example, we could ask if the model is biased against LGBTQ words, such as the word '*homosexual*' compared to the word '*straight*'? One way to provide an answer to such a question is to evaluate a large number of contexts, replacing a word in the original context with the words '*homosexual*' and '*straight*'. Doing that however is prohibitive with large text classification models. If an interpretation method can do this in a reasonable time and accuracy, it enables a user access to model behavior across a large number of contexts.

Considering the preceding requirements, we propose MOXIE (MOdeling conteXt-sensitive InfluencE of words) to enable a reliable interface for a user to query a neural network based text classification model beyond model predictions. In MOXIE, we aim to learn the context-sensitive influence of words (see Figure 1 for the overall architecture). We show that learning this objective enables answers to the aforementioned questions (Section 3.2). Further, having a global learning objective provides an automatic way to test the interpretation method as a whole and improve it using the standard ML pipeline (Section 3.3). We evaluate the reliability and efficiency of MOXIE on the task of sentiment analysis (Section 4)[4].

2 Related Work

Word importance scores have been a popular area of research for interpreting text classifiers, including gradient based methods (Wallace et al., 2019), using nearest neighbors (Wallace et al., 2018), intrinsic model-provided scores such as attention (Wiegreffe and Pinter, 2019), and scores learned through perturbations of the test example (Ribeiro et al., 2016). There has also been effort to expand the scope to phrases (Murdoch et al., 2018), as well as provide hierarchical importance scores (Chen et al., 2020). However these methods tend to derive from an underlying heuristic applicable at the example level to get the importance scores. With

[3]The need for going beyond importance scores has also been realized and explored for user-centric explainable AI interface design (Liao et al., 2020).

[4]Note that we are not claiming to build inherently faithful mechanisms, but ones which allow inherent testing of their faithfulness. For example, a counterfactual or a bias prediction can be tested by the model under interpretation (see Section 4).

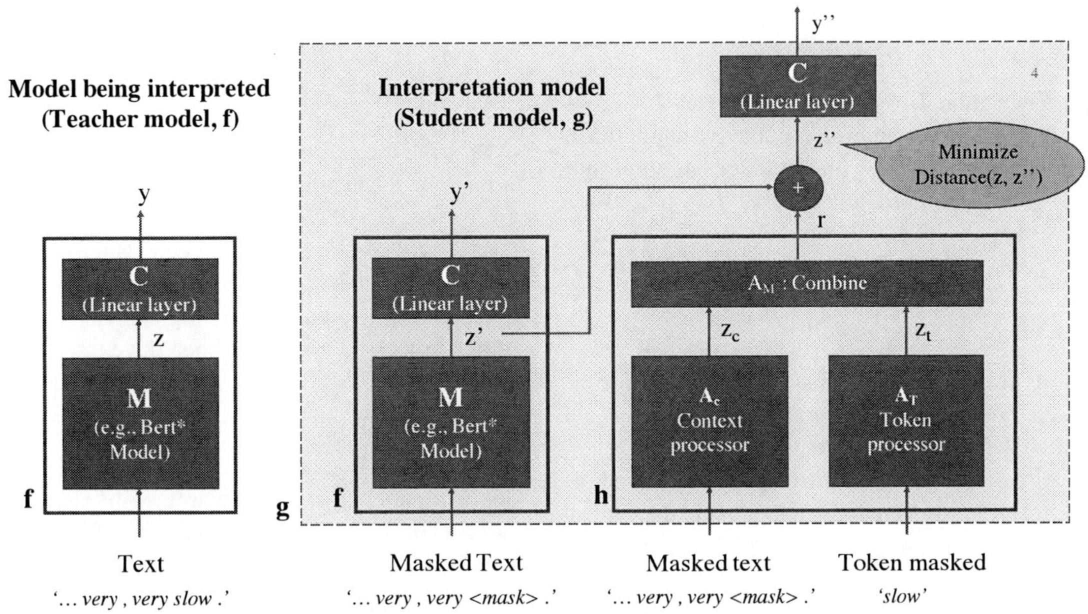

Figure 1: *Overall architecture of MOXIE*: The model being interpreted (f) which we call the teacher model is shown on the left. It processes an input text such as '... *very very slow*' to produce a representation z through module M and label scores y through a linear classification layer C. When presented with the same input but the word '*slow*' masked, it produces outputs z' and y' respectively. We learn the difference in the two representations ($z - z'$) as a proxy for the context-sensitive influence of the word '*slow*' in the student model (g). This is done by processing the masked context and the token masked through arbitrarily complex modules A_C and A_T which produce fixed length representations z_c and z_t respectively. The combine module (A_M) takes these as input to produce the output r. We learn by minimizing the mean square error between z and $z'' = z' + r$. Keeping the combine module shallow allows the processing of a large number of tokens for a given context and vice versa in a reasonable time. Please see Section 3.1 for details on the architecture and Section 3.2 for how this architecture enables answers to the motivating questions.

perturbation methods, where a locally valid classifier is learned near the test example (Ribeiro et al., 2016), there is a hyperparameter dependence as well as stochasticity at the level of test examples.

While it's not inherently problematic to use such heuristics, it makes it hard to improve upon the method, as we need to rely on indirect measures to evaluate the method. Further, recent work has shown that the skepticism in the existing methods is valid and important (Ghorbani et al., 2019). In this work, we use a global learning objective which allows us to make predictions of importance scores.

Apart from word importance scores, explanation by example style method have been studied (Han et al., 2020). Like word importance based methods, however, these methods don't provide a clear recipe for further analysis of the model. In this work, we aim to produce testable predictions such as counterfactuals and potential biases.

Measuring faithfulness of an interpretation model can be hard. Jacovi and Goldberg (2020) suggest that human evaluation shouldn't be used. In this work, we circumvent the hard problem of evaluating the faithfulness of an interpretation method by making it output predictions which can be tested by the model being interpreted.

3 MOXIE

The overall architecture employed to learn MOXIE is shown in Figure 1. We introduce the notation and describe the architecture in detail in Section 3.1. In Section 3.2, we discuss how MOXIE provides answers to the motivating questions.

3.1 Notation and Architecture

Let x denote a text sequence $x_1 x_2 ... x_n$. We denote by x^i_{mask} the same sequence but the ith token x_i replaced by a mask token: $x_1 x_2 \ldots x_{i-1} \langle \text{mask} \rangle x_{i+1} \ldots x_n$.

In the following, we refer to the model being

interpreted as the teacher model and the learned interpretation model as the student model.

Teacher model: The teacher model f is composed of a representation module M and a linear classification layer C, and produces a representation $z = M(x)$ and label scores $y = C(z)$ for a text input x. The label prediction is obtained as the label with the highest score: $l = \mathrm{argmax}(y)$. We believe this covers a fairly general class of text classifiers: $y = f(x) = C(M(x)) = C(z)$.

Student model: With mask token $\mathrm{mask_t}$ for the teacher model, we create masked input $x^i_{\mathrm{mask_t}}$ for which the teacher model outputs $z'_i = M(x^i_{\mathrm{mask_t}})$.

As a proxy for the context-sensitive influence of the token x_i, we aim to model $z - z'_i$ in the student model. For this, we use the following submodules:

- **Context processor** A_C processes masked text to produce a context representation. In particular, with mask token $\mathrm{mask_s}$ for the context processor, we create the masked input $x^i_{\mathrm{mask_s}}$ for which the context processor outputs $z_{c,i} = A_C(x^i_{\mathrm{mask_s}})$. Note that the mask token could be different for the teacher model and the context processor. We fine-tune a pre-trained roberta-base (Liu et al., 2019) model to learn the context processor, where we take the output at the mask token position as $z_{c,i}$.
- **Token processor** A_T processes the token which was masked to produce representation $z_{t,i} = A_T(x_i)$. Note that we can mask spans as well with the same architecture, where x_i denotes a span of tokens instead of one. For all our experiments, we fine-tune a pre-trained RoBERTa-base model to learn the token processor, where we take the output at the first token position as $z_{t,i}$.
- **Combine** module A_M combines the outputs from the context and token processors to produce representation r.

In summary, the sub-module h takes the input x and token location i to produce output r_i:

$$r_i = h(x, i) = A_M(A_C(x^i_{\mathrm{mask_s}}), A_T(x_i)) \quad (1)$$

To get label predictions, we add z'_i to r_i and feed it to the teacher model classification layer C. In summary, the student model g takes as input x and token location i to make predictions y''_i:

$$y''_i = g(x, i) = C(z'_i + h(x, i)) = C(z'_i + r_i) \quad (2)$$

Modules h and g provide token influence and label scores respectively. We learn the parameters of the student model by minimizing the mean square error between z and z''_i.

Keeping the combine module shallow is crucial as it allows evaluating a large number of tokens in a given context and vice versa quickly (Section 3.2). For all our experiments, we first concatenate $z_{c,i} + z_{t,i}$, $z_{c,i} - z_{t,i}$ and $z_{c,i} \odot z_{t,i}$ to obtain z_{concat}, where $\odot$ represents element wise multiplication. $z_{\mathrm{concat},i}$ is then processed using two linear layers:

$$A_M(z_{c,i}, z_{t,i}) = W_2(\tanh(W_1 z_{\mathrm{concat},i} + b_1)) + b_2 \quad (3)$$

where W_1, b_1, W_2, and b_2 are learnable parameters. The parameter sizes are constrained by the input and output dimensions and assuming W_1 to be a square matrix.

3.2 Using MOXIE

3.2.1 Importance Scores

MOXIE provides two kinds of token-level scores. **Influence scores** can be obtained from predictions of the sub-module h, $r_i = h(x, i)$:

$$\hat{s}_i = \mathrm{softmax}(C(r_i)) \quad (4)$$

For binary classification, we map the score to the range $[-1, 1]$ and select the score of the positive label: $s_i = 2 * \hat{s}_i[+\mathrm{ve}] + 1$. The sign of the score s_i can then be interpreted as indicative of the sentiment (positive or negative), while its magnitude indicates the strength of the influence.

Unlike ratios aim to give an estimate of the ratio of words in the vocabulary which when used to replace a token lead to a different prediction. The student model architecture allows us to pre-compute and store token representations through the token processor (A_T) for a large vocabulary, and evaluate the impact each token in the vocabulary might have in a given context. This requires running the context processor and the teacher model only once. Let V be a vocabulary of words, then for each word w^j, we can pre-compute and store token embeddings E_V such that $E^j_V = A_T(w^j)$. For example x with label l, teacher model representations z and z'_i for the full and masked input, and context processor output $z_{c,i}$, the unlike ratio u_i can be computed as:

$$\begin{aligned} r_{V,i} &= A_M(z_{c,i}, E_V) \\ y_{V,i} &= C(z + r_{V,i}) \\ u_i &= \frac{|\{w : w \in V, \mathrm{argmax}(y_{V,i}) \neq l\}|}{|V|} \end{aligned} \quad (5)$$

If the unlike ratio u_i for a token x_i is 0, it would imply that the model prediction is completely determined by the rest of the context. On the other hand, an unlike ratio close to 1.0 would indicate that the word x_i is important for the prediction as replacing it with any word is likely to change the decision. In this work we restrict the vocabulary V using the part-of-speech (POS) tag of the token in consideration (see Appendix C for details).

Finally, getting **phrase-level scores** is easy with MOXIE when the student model is trained by masking spans and not just words.

Please see Section 4.3 for details and evaluation.

3.2.2 Counterfactuals

As discussed in the preceding section, the student model allows making predictions for a large number of token replacements for a given context. As before, we restrict the vocabulary of possible replacements using the POS tag of the token in consideration. To generate potential counterfactuals, we get predictions from the student model for all replacements and select the ones with label predictions different from the teacher model's label. Please see Section 4.4 for details and evaluation.

3.2.3 Biases

Modeling the context-sensitive influence of words in MOXIE enables analyzing the effect of a word in a large number of contexts. We can pre-compute and store representations for a large number of contexts using the teacher model and the context processor of the student model. Given a query word, we can then analyze how it influences the predictions across different contexts. Pairwise queries, i.e., queries involving two words can reveal relative biases against a word compared to the other. Please see Section 4.5 for details and evaluation.

3.3 Improving the Interpretation Method

The student model g introduced in the preceding section is expected to approximate the teacher model f, and the accuracy of the same can be measured easily (see Section 4.2). We expect that as this accuracy increases, the answers to the preceding questions will become more reliable. Thus, MOXIE provides a straightforward way to improve itself. The standard ML pipeline involving testing on a held-out set can be employed.

4 Experiments

We aim to answer the following questions:

Q1 How well does the student model approximate the teacher model? (Section 4.2)

Q2 How does MOXIE compare with methods which access test example neighborhoods to generate importance scores? (Section 4.3)

Q3 Can MOXIE reliably produce counterfactuals? (Section 4.4)

Q4 Can MOXIE predict potential biases against certain words? (Section 4.5)

We use the task of binary sentiment classification on the Stanford Sentiment Treebank-2 (SST-2) dataset (Socher et al., 2013; Wang et al., 2018) for training and evaluation. In Section 4.1.2, we provide text preprocessing details. We evaluate the student model accuracy against the teacher model (Q1) across four models: bert-base-cased (Devlin et al., 2019), roberta-base (Liu et al., 2019), xlmr-base (Conneau et al., 2019), RoBERTa-large (Liu et al., 2019). For the rest of the evaluation, we use RoBERTa-base as the teacher model. We use the Hugging Face transformers library v3.0.2 (Wolf et al., 2019) for our experiments.

4.1 Experimental Setup

4.1.1 Training Details

As models to be interpreted (teacher models), we fine-tuned bert-base-cased, RoBERTa-base, xlmr-base and RoBERTa-large on the SST-2 train set. We trained each model for 3 epochs.

For the interpretation models (student models), we initialize the context processor and token processor with a pre-trained RoBERTa-base model. We then train the context processor, token processor and combine module parameters jointly for 10 epochs with model selection using dev set (using all-correct accuracy, see Section 4.2 for details).

For both teacher and student models, we use the AdamW (Loshchilov and Hutter, 2018) optimizer with an initial learning rate of $2e-5$ (see Appendix A for other training details).

For all experiments, for training, we generate context-token pairs by masking spans obtained from a constituency parser (the span masked is fed to the token processor). For all evaluation, we use a word tokenizer unless otherwise specified. Training with spans compared to words didn't lead to much difference in the overall results (as measured in Section 4.2), and we retained the span version to potentially enable phrase level scores.

Model	Teacher baseline (Context-only)	Student Model (Context &Token)
bert-base-cased	73.48	87.64
RoBERTa-base	78.64	89.24
xlmr-base	74.08	86.93
RoBERTa-large	82.37	89.74

Table 2: *Evaluation of the student model and a context-only teacher baseline against teacher model predictions on the test set* using the all-correct accuracy metric. The context-only teacher model baseline does better than chance but the student model provides gains across all teacher models. This indicates that the student model learns context-token interactions. Please see Section 4.2 for details.

Text: it 's a charming and often affecting journey **Prediction:** +ve **Top 2 scores:** charming (0.38), affecting (0.12)
Text: unflinchingly bleak and desperate **Prediction**: -ve **Top 2 scores:** bleak (-0.99), desperate (-0.92)
Text: allows us to hope that nolan is posed to embark a major career as a commercial yet inventive filmmaker . **Prediction:** +ve **Top 2 scores:** allows (0.97), inventive (0.91)

Table 3: *Word importance scores* on the first three dev set examples. Top two scores are shown.

4.1.2 Tokenization and POS Tagging

We use the nltk (Bird et al., 2009) tokenizer for getting word level tokens. For training by masking spans, we obtain spans from benepar (Kitaev and Klein, 2018), a constituency parser plugin for nltk. We use nltk's averaged_perceptron_tagger for obtaining POS tags, and use the universal_tagset.

4.2 Evaluating Student Model on the Test Set

In this section, we measure how well the student model approximates the teacher model. The student model provides a prediction at the token level: $g(x, i)$. We define an example level **all-correct accuracy** metric: the set of predictions for an example are considered correct only if all predictions match the reference label.

As a baseline, we consider token level predictions from the teacher model obtained from masked contexts: $f(x^i_{\text{mask}_t})$. If the student model improves over this baseline, it would suggest having learned context-token interactions and not just using the contexts for making predictions.

In Table 2, we show all-correct accuracies of the baseline and the student model on the test set. The baseline does better than chance but the student model provides significant gains over it. This indicates that the student model learns context-token interactions and is not relying on the context alone.

Text: in exactly 89 minutes , most of which passed as slowly as if i 'd been sitting naked on an igloo , formula 51 sank from quirky to jerky to utter turkey . (-ve) **Prediction:** -ve **Top 2 word-level scores:** quirky (0.26), formula (-0.22) **Top 2 phrase-level scores:** to utter turkey (-0.35), quirky (0.26)

Table 4: *Word and Phrase importance scores* on an example selected from the first 10 dev set examples.

A key advantage of MOXIE is providing a way to improve upon itself. We believe improvements in the all-correct accuracy of the student model would lead to improved performance when evaluated as in the subsequent sections. For completion, we provide the accuracies of the student model against gold labels in Appendix B.

4.3 Importance Scores

Table 3 capture the importance scores on the first three dev set examples. Table 4 shows an example selected from the first 10 dev set examples demonstrating how MOXIE can produce meaningful phrase-level scores.

As discussed before, it's hard to evaluate importance scores for trustworthiness. We evaluate the trustworthiness of MOXIE in subsequent sections. Here, we aim to contrast MOXIE, which doesn't learn its parameters using test examples, with methods which do. We aim to devise a test which would benefit the latter and see how well MOXIE performs. We choose LIME (Ribeiro et al., 2016) which directly incorporates the knowledge of teacher model predictions when words in the input text are modified. To test the same, we start with test examples where the teacher model makes an error, and successively mask words using importance scores, with an aim to correct the label prediction. With a masking budget, we compute the number of tokens that need masking. We report on: **Coverage**, the % of examples for which the model decision could be changed, and **Average length masked**, the average number of words that needed masking (see Appendix D for detailed steps). The test favors LIME as LIME learns using teacher model predictions on the test example and its neighborhood while MOXIE learns only on the train set.

We compare against LIME and a Random baseline where we assign random importance scores to the words in the input. From MOXIE, we obtain

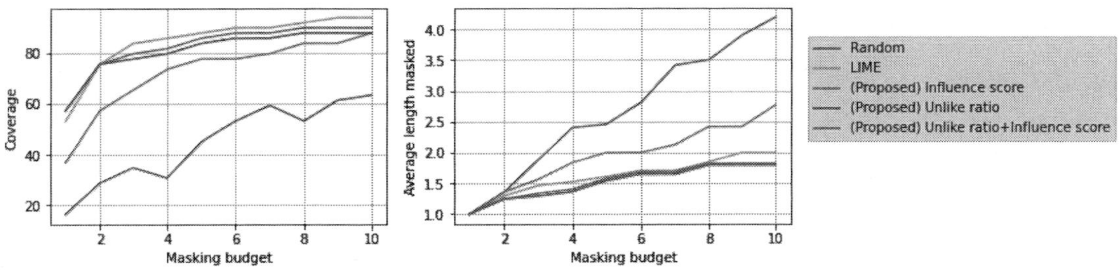

Figure 2: *Evaluation of importance scores* on examples where the teacher model makes an error. Tokens are successively masked using importance scores until the masking budget is met or the prediction of the teacher model changes. We report on the coverage and the average length that needed masking when the decision could be changed. We note that all methods perform better than the random baseline. MOXIE competes with LIME despite not seeing the test example and its neighborhood during training. Please see Section 4.3 for details.

influence scores and unlike ratios. We also derive a hybrid score (Unlike ratio+influence score) by using unlike ratios with influence scores as back-off when the former are non-informative (e.g., all scores are 0). Figure 2 captures the results of this test on the 49 dev set examples where the teacher model prediction was wrong.

We note that all scores are better than the random baseline. Influence scores do worse than LIME but unlike ratios and the hybrid scores are competitive with LIME. This is despite never seeing the test example neighborhood during training, unlike LIME. The results support the hypothesis that a global learning objective can provide effective importance scores. However, this is not the main contribution of this paper. Our aim is to enable increased interaction with the model by providing testable predictions as discussed in subsequent sections.

4.4 Counterfactuals

As discussed in the Section 3.2.2, MOXIE allows predictions of counterfactuals using pre-computed token embeddings. We show examples of generated counterfactuals in Appendix E.1. We evaluate the reliability of the generated counterfactuals by computing the accuracy of the top-10 predictions using the teacher model. The student model takes a pre-computed POS-tagged dictionary of token embeddings (obtained using token processor A_T) and a context as input and predicts the top-10 candidate replacements (see Appendix E.2 for details).

Figure 3 captures the counterfactual accuracies obtained across contexts (with at least one counterfactual) in the dev set. Out of 872 examples, 580 examples had at least one context for which the student model made counterfactual predictions. In total, there were 1823 contexts with counterfactuals. The median counterfactual accuracy across contexts with at least one counterfactual was 90% which is significantly higher than chance.

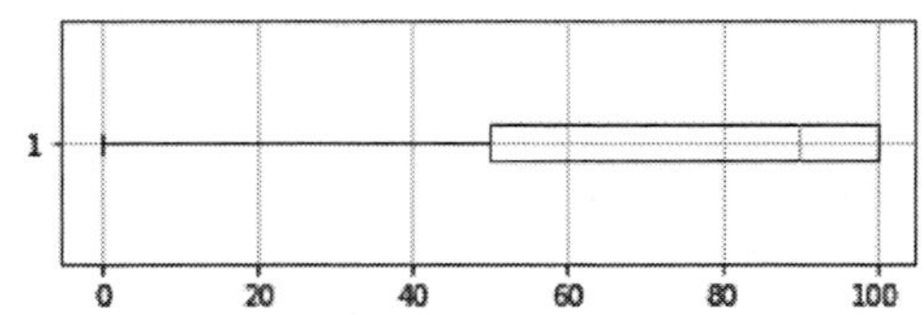

Figure 3: *Counterfactual prediction accuracies*: across contexts for which at least one counterfactual was found. The box indicates the range between quartiles 1 & 3. The median accuracy was 90.0% which is better than chance. This indicates that MOXIE is capable of reliably predicting counterfactuals. Please see Section 4.4 for details.

4.5 Biases

As discussed in the Section 3.2.3, MOXIE can quickly process a large number of contexts for a given word. As a case study, we look for potential biases against LGBTQ words in the teacher model.

We make pairwise queries to the student model, with a pair of words: a control word and a probe word, where we expect task specific meaning to not change between these words. We require the student model to find contexts from an input dataset where the control word leads to a positive sentiment prediction but the probe word leads to a negative sentiment prediction. We use the training dataset as the input dataset.

To avoid any negative influence from other parts of the context, we further require that the original context (as present in the input dataset) lead to a positive sentiment by the teacher model. Finally, we remove negative contexts, e.g., the context '*The*

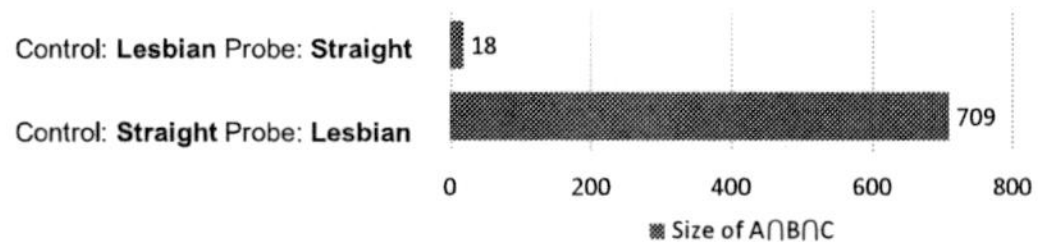

Figure 4: *Measuring potential biases*: using the student model. We show the relative sizes of the sets obtained with positive predictions with control word but negative predictions with the probe word. The results indicate a potential bias against the word '*lesbian*' compared to the word '*straight*' (see Section 4.5)

*movie is not **bad***' would be positive despite '*bad*' clearly having a negative influence. To ease the bias analysis by remove such contexts, we can remove all sentences with words which tend to be negative, e.g., *not*, *never* etc. For adjective contexts, we use the student model to filter out such contexts using a list of clearly positive/negative adjectives (see Appendix F for details on pre-processing contexts).

The output of the preceding steps can be pre-computed and stored. Next, we find the set of contexts satisfying the following criteria (e.g., with control word '*straight*' and probe word '*lesbian*'):

$\mathbf{S_1}$ Teacher model predicts positive on the original context (pre-computed and stored), e.g., x:'*I have **cool** friends*', $\operatorname{argmax}(f(x)) = +ve$.

$\mathbf{S_2}$ Student model predicts positive when the marked token is replaced with the control word, e.g., x_{control}:'*I have **straight** friends*', $\operatorname{argmax}(g(x_{\text{control}}, i)) = +ve$.

$\mathbf{S_3}$ Student model predicts negative when the marked token is replaced with the probe word, e.g., x_{probe}: '*I have **lesbian** friends*', $\operatorname{argmax}(g(x_{\text{probe}}, i)) = -ve$.

S_2 and S_3 can be computed efficiently by pre-computing the output of the context processor A_C for all contexts in the input dataset. If E_C denotes the matrix of output embeddings from the context processor, S_2 and S_3 for word w can be computed by first obtaining the token processor representation $z_t = A_T(w)$ and then using the combine module $y_C = C(A_M(E_C, z_t))$.

The relative size of the set $S_1 \cap S_2 \cap S_3$ is indicative of a potential bias against the probe word. Figure 4 shows the size of the set $S_1 \cap S_2 \cap S_3$ with '*straight*' and '*lesbian*' interchangeably as control and probe words. Note that the relative size with probe word as '*lesbian*' is much larger than the

almost every **lesbian** facet of production
gay to its animatronic roots
the **bisexual** lives of the characters in his film
the most **transsexual** thing about this film

Table 5: *Examples of biased contexts (negative prediction).* If the highlighted word were to be swapped by the word '*straight*', the prediction would be positive. See Section 4.5 for details.

Size of $S_1 \cap S_2 \cap S_3$ (top-100)	Control word	Acc	Probe word	Acc
100	straight	67.0	lesbian	90.0
100	straight	61.0	gay	93.0
100	straight	68.0	bisexual	82.0
100	straight	69.0	transsexual	85.0
0	straight	-	queer	-

Table 6: *Evaluating student model claims of biases*: Up to 100 confident contexts are selected using student model predictions where the student model claims a +ve prediction using the control word and -ve prediction using the probe word. The predictions are tested using the teacher model and the accuracy reported. Note that except for '*queer*' where the set size is zero, the prediction accuracy of the student model is better than chance. This indicates the ability of the student model to predict biases. See Section 4.5 for details.

relative size with probe word as '*straight*'. This is indicative of a potential bias against the word '*lesbian*'. Table 5 shows some examples of biased sentences obtained through this procedure.

Next, we aim to evaluate the claim of the student model using the teacher model. For this, we consider the set $S_1 \cap S_2 \cap S_3$ with probe word as '*lesbian*' and evaluate the contexts with both '*straight*' and '*lesbian*'. The student model claims the model prediction to be positive for the former and negative for the latter. We process the examples with the corresponding replacements using the teacher model to measure the accuracy of this claim (i.e., teacher model's outputs serve as the reference label). The accuracy of the student model claim with '*straight*' is 65.16% while with '*lesbian*', it is 75.88%. We also evaluate the 100 most confident predictions from the student model (using softmax scores). The accuracies with '*straight*' and '*lesbian*' then increase to 67.0% and 90.0% respectively. In Table 6, we show the results on the 100 most confident predictions for more LGBTQ words. Note that we don't claim this to be an exhaustive set of words reflecting the LGBTQ community, but as only roughly representative. The results indicate a similar pattern as with '*lesbian*', except for the word '*queer*' where the student model doesn't predict any biased contexts. This is presumably due to the word '*queer*' carrying additional meanings, unlike the other LGBTQ words.

Finally, the student model provides ~450 speedup when compared to using the teacher model to probe for biases. It takes less than $1s$ to test a control word against a probe word on a single NVIDIA V100 GPU using the student model, thus enabling an interactive interface. Unlike using the teacher model directly, MOXIE allows precomputing large sets of context/token representations and thus obtain the aforementioned gains.

In summary, the results indicate bias against LGBTQ words. The evaluation indicates that the student model can make reliable bias predictions.

5 Conclusion

In summary, we have shown that MOXIE provides a novel framework for interpreting text classifiers and a method to draw quick insights about the model on large datasets. MOXIE can make efficient, testable and reliable predictions beyond importance score, such as counterfactuals and potential biases. Further, with a global learning objective, it provides a clear path for improving itself using the standard ML pipeline. Finally, the principles and the evaluation methodology should help the interpretability research overcome the problem of testing the faithfulness of interpretation methods.

As future work, we identify improving the accuracy of the student model. Further analysis of the nature of counterfactuals selected by the student model could lead to useful insights towards improving the interpretation method. Finally, identifying other learning objectives which enable testable predictions would be useful and challenging.

6 Broader Impact

In this work, we aim to improve interpretability of existing text classification systems. More interpretable systems are likely to reveal biases and help towards a fairer deployment of production systems built using these systems.

To demonstrate our work, we choose to study potential biases against words associated with the LGBTQ community. In particular, we probe for bias in a learned sentiment classification systems against the words that make up the acronym LGBTQ - Lesbian, Gay, Bisexual, Transsexual and Queer. Note that we don't use identity information of any individual for this. Instead, we probe whether, in arbitrary contexts, the learned sentiment classification model is likely to find these qualifiers more negative when compared to adjectives in general or adjectives usually associated with the hegemony. Our work doesn't aim to discriminate but instead provides a way to measure if there are intended or unintended biases in a learned system.

Acknowledgements

We would like to thank the reviewers for their valuable feedback.

References

Pepa Atanasova, Jakob Grue Simonsen, Christina Lioma, and Isabelle Augenstein. 2020. A diagnostic study of explainability techniques for text classification. In *Proceedings of the 2020 Conference on Empirical Methods in Natural Language Processing (EMNLP)*, pages 3256–3274, Online. Association for Computational Linguistics.

Steven Bird, Ewan Klein, and Edward Loper. 2009. *Natural language processing with Python: analyzing text with the natural language toolkit*. " O'Reilly Media, Inc.".

Hanjie Chen, Guangtao Zheng, and Yangfeng Ji. 2020. Generating hierarchical explanations on text classification via feature interaction detection. In *Proceedings of the 58th Annual Meeting of the Association for Computational Linguistics*, pages 5578–5593, Online. Association for Computational Linguistics.

Alexis Conneau, Kartikay Khandelwal, Naman Goyal, Vishrav Chaudhary, Guillaume Wenzek, Francisco Guzmán, Edouard Grave, Myle Ott, Luke Zettlemoyer, and Veselin Stoyanov. 2019. Unsupervised cross-lingual representation learning at scale. *arXiv preprint arXiv:1911.02116*.

Jacob Devlin, Ming-Wei Chang, Kenton Lee, and Kristina Toutanova. 2019. BERT: Pre-training of deep bidirectional transformers for language understanding. In *Proceedings of the 2019 Conference of the North American Chapter of the Association for Computational Linguistics: Human Language Technologies, Volume 1 (Long and Short Papers)*, pages 4171–4186, Minneapolis, Minnesota. Association for Computational Linguistics.

Amirata Ghorbani, Abubakar Abid, and James Zou. 2019. Interpretation of neural networks is fragile. In *Proceedings of the AAAI Conference on Artificial Intelligence*, volume 33, pages 3681–3688.

Xiaochuang Han, Byron C. Wallace, and Yulia Tsvetkov. 2020. Explaining black box predictions and unveiling data artifacts through influence functions. In *Proceedings of the 58th Annual Meeting of the Association for Computational Linguistics*, pages 5553–5563, Online. Association for Computational Linguistics.

Alon Jacovi and Yoav Goldberg. 2020. Towards faithfully interpretable NLP systems: How should we define and evaluate faithfulness? In *Proceedings of the 58th Annual Meeting of the Association for Computational Linguistics*, pages 4198–4205, Online. Association for Computational Linguistics.

Nikita Kitaev and Dan Klein. 2018. Constituency parsing with a self-attentive encoder. In *Proceedings of the 56th Annual Meeting of the Association for Computational Linguistics (Volume 1: Long Papers)*, pages 2676–2686, Melbourne, Australia. Association for Computational Linguistics.

Q Vera Liao, Daniel Gruen, and Sarah Miller. 2020. Questioning the ai: informing design practices for explainable ai user experiences. In *Proceedings of the 2020 CHI Conference on Human Factors in Computing Systems*, pages 1–15.

Zachary C Lipton. 2018. The mythos of model interpretability. *Queue*, 16(3):31–57.

Yinhan Liu, Myle Ott, Naman Goyal, Jingfei Du, Mandar Joshi, Danqi Chen, Omer Levy, Mike Lewis, Luke Zettlemoyer, and Veselin Stoyanov. 2019. Roberta: A robustly optimized bert pretraining approach. *arXiv preprint arXiv:1907.11692*.

Ilya Loshchilov and Frank Hutter. 2018. Decoupled weight decay regularization. In *International Conference on Learning Representations*.

W James Murdoch, Peter J Liu, and Bin Yu. 2018. Beyond word importance: Contextual decomposition to extract interactions from lstms. In *International Conference on Learning Representations*.

Colin Raffel, Noam Shazeer, Adam Roberts, Katherine Lee, Sharan Narang, Michael Matena, Yanqi Zhou, Wei Li, and Peter J Liu. 2019. Exploring the limits of transfer learning with a unified text-to-text transformer. *arXiv preprint arXiv:1910.10683*.

Marco Tulio Ribeiro, Sameer Singh, and Carlos Guestrin. 2016. " why should i trust you?" explaining the predictions of any classifier. In *Proceedings of the 22nd ACM SIGKDD international conference on knowledge discovery and data mining*, pages 1135–1144.

Richard Socher, Alex Perelygin, Jean Wu, Jason Chuang, Christopher D. Manning, Andrew Ng, and Christopher Potts. 2013. Recursive deep models for semantic compositionality over a sentiment treebank. In *Proceedings of the 2013 Conference on Empirical Methods in Natural Language Processing*, pages 1631–1642, Seattle, Washington, USA. Association for Computational Linguistics.

Mukund Sundararajan, Ankur Taly, and Qiqi Yan. 2017. Axiomatic attribution for deep networks. In *International Conference on Machine Learning*, pages 3319–3328. PMLR.

Eric Wallace, Shi Feng, and Jordan Boyd-Graber. 2018. Interpreting neural networks with nearest neighbors. In *Proceedings of the 2018 EMNLP Workshop BlackboxNLP: Analyzing and Interpreting Neural Networks for NLP*, pages 136–144, Brussels, Belgium. Association for Computational Linguistics.

Eric Wallace, Jens Tuyls, Junlin Wang, Sanjay Subramanian, Matt Gardner, and Sameer Singh. 2019. AllenNLP interpret: A framework for explaining predictions of NLP models. In *Proceedings of the 2019 Conference on Empirical Methods in Natural Language Processing and the 9th International Joint Conference on Natural Language Processing (EMNLP-IJCNLP): System Demonstrations*, pages 7–12, Hong Kong, China. Association for Computational Linguistics.

Alex Wang, Amanpreet Singh, Julian Michael, Felix Hill, Omer Levy, and Samuel R Bowman. 2018. Glue: A multi-task benchmark and analysis platform for natural language understanding. In *International Conference on Learning Representations*.

Sarah Wiegreffe and Yuval Pinter. 2019. Attention is not not explanation. *arXiv preprint arXiv:1908.04626*.

Thomas Wolf, Lysandre Debut, Victor Sanh, Julien Chaumond, Clement Delangue, Anthony Moi, Pierric Cistac, Tim Rault, Rémi Louf, Morgan Funtowicz, Joe Davison, Sam Shleifer, Patrick von Platen, Clara Ma, Yacine Jernite, Julien Plu, Canwen Xu, Teven Le Scao, Sylvain Gugger, Mariama Drame, Quentin Lhoest, and Alexander M. Rush. 2019. Huggingface's transformers: State-of-the-art natural language processing. *ArXiv*, abs/1910.03771.

A Training Details

A.1 Data

The SST-2 dataset (Socher et al., 2013; Wang et al., 2018) contains English language movie reviews from the "Rotten Tomatoes" website. The training data consists of 67349 examples and is roughly label-balanced with 56% positive label and 44% negative label data. The dev and test sets contain 872 and 1821 examples respectively.

A.2 Other Training Details

For the teacher models, we train the models for 3 epochs. For optimization, we use an initial learning rate of 2e-5, adam epsilon of 1e-8, max gradient norm of 1.0 and a batch size of 64. The maximum token length for a text example was set to 128.

	Teacher Model (accuracy)	Student Model (All-correct accuracy)
bert-base-cased	91.97	85.09
roberta-base	94.38	86.93
xlmr-base	92.55	83.37
roberta-large	95.64	88.88

Table 7: *Accuracy against gold labels* on the dev set. The student model does significantly better than chance with scope for improvement.

POS tag	Size of extracted vocabulary
NOUN	7534
VERB	2749
ADJ	3394
ADV	809
.	15
DET	26
ADP	79
CONJ	12
PRT	19
PRON	28

Table 8: *Size of extracted lists of POS-tagged words.*

For student models, we train the models for 10 epochs. For optimization, we use an initial learning rate of 2e-5, adam epsilon of 1e-8, max gradient norm of 1.0 and a batch size of 64. The maximum token length for a text example was set to 128. The maximum token length of the masked span input to the token processor was set to 50. When trained on Nvidia's GeForce GTX 1080 Ti GPUs, each run took approximately 6 hours to complete.

B Evaluating Student Model against Gold Labels

In Table 7, we provide the accuracies of the teacher and student models against gold labels. In this work, we care about accuracies of the student model against teacher model predictions and we show accuracies against gold labels here only for completion.

C Pre-computing POS-tagged Dictionary of Token Embeddings

For evaluating importance scores and counterfactual predictions, we use a POS-tagged dictionary of token embeddings. The token embeddings are obtained by processing the tokens through the token processor A_T. This is done only once for a given student model and used for all subsequent experiments.

We use the training dataset for extracting the list of open class words. We use nltk's averaged_perceptron_tagger for obtaining POS tags, and use the universal_tagset[5]. The open class words correspond to the tags — *NOUN, VERB, ADJ, ADV*. We assign each word to the POS tag with which it occurs most commonly in the training dataset.

For closed class words, we use the Penn Treebank corpus included in the ntlk toolkit (*treebank*). Again, we use the universal_tagset from nltk toolkit. We ignore the *NUM* and *X* as well as open class tags. For the punctuation tag, we remove any token containing alphanumeric characters.

In Table 8, we show the size of the extracted lists for each POS tag.

Input: A text sequence x: $x_1 x_2 ... x_n$
Input: Importance scores s: $s_1 s_2 ... s_n$
Input: A masking budget m
Output: The number of words that need masking
Initialize: count $\leftarrow -1$; $a \leftarrow x$
Compute teacher prediction:
  prediction $\leftarrow \text{argmax}(f(a))$
Sort importance scores:
  ImportanceOrder $\leftarrow \text{argsort}(s)$
for $k \leftarrow 1$ ***to*** m **do**
  $i \leftarrow \text{ImportanceOrder}(k)$
  Mask the next important word: $a \leftarrow a^i_{\text{mask\_t}}$
  Compute teacher prediction: $l = \text{argmax}(f(a))$
  if $l \neq$ prediction **then**
    Set count if criterion met: count $\leftarrow k$
    return count
  end
end
return count

Algorithm 1: MASKLENGTH Computes the number of words that need masking to change the model prediction

D Importance Scores

D.1 Evaluating Importance Scores

In Algorithm 1, we provide the detailed steps for computing the mask length as used in the evaluation of importance scores.

Unlike ratios are computed using the pre-computed POS-tagged dictionary of token embeddings obtained as in Section C.

In Table 9, we show the top-3 importance scores supporting the prediction from the model being interpreted, obtained from LIME and MOXIE on the first 4 dev set examples where the model being interpreted makes an error (wrong label pre-

[5]The meaning and examples of the tags in the universal tagset can be found in the nltk book https://www.nltk.org/book/ch05.html

Text: the iditarod lasts for days - this just felt like it did . **Gold label:**-ve **Prediction:**+ve **LIME:** did (0.24), lasts (0.19), it (0.13) **MOXIE influence scores:** days (0.88), like (0.82), the (0.77) **MOXIE unlike ratios:** for (78.48), did (63.26), like (41.77)
Text: holden caulfield did it better . **Gold label:**-ve **Prediction:**+ve **LIME:** better (0.03), it (0.02), holden (0.01) **MOXIE influence scores:** better (0.97), . (0.93), did (0.93) **MOXIE unlike ratios:** holden (22.54), caulfield (17.61), better (12.36)
Text: you wo n't like roger , but you will quickly recognize him . **Gold label:**-ve **Prediction:**+ve **LIME:** recognize (0.20), but (0.19), will (0.14) **MOXIE influence scores:** quickly (0.98), but (0.93), n't (0.68) **MOXIE unlike ratios:** recognize (12.62), quickly (3.58), will (0.54)
Text: if steven soderbergh 's ' solaris ' is a failure^a it is a glorious failure^b . **Gold label:**+ve **Prediction:**-ve **LIME:** failure^a (-0.91), failure^b (-0.91), if (-0.03) **MOXIE influence scores:** failure^b (-1.00), a (-0.56), if (-0.36) **MOXIE unlike ratios:** failure^b (30.33)

Table 9: *Word importance scores when the model to be interpreted makes a wrong prediction* The top three scores supporting the model prediction obtained using LIME and MOXIE are shown for the first 4 dev set examples where the model being interpreted makes an error. For MOXIE, we show scores obtained using influence scores as well as unlike ratios. Superscripts are used to distinguish word positions if required.

diction). For MOXIE, we show importance scores obtained using both influence scores and unlike ratios. MOXIE scores are position independent and we assign the same scores to all occurrences of a word.

E Counterfactuals

E.1 Example Counterfactual Predictions

In Table 10, we show selected examples of counterfactual predictions. The examples have been picked from the first 10 dev set examples.

Text (Prediction)	Replacement Prediction
unflinchingly **bleak** and desperate (-ve)	sensual
it 's **slow** – very , very slow . (-ve)	enjoyable
a sometimes **tedious** film (-ve)	heart-breaking

Table 10: *Example counterfactual predictions* selected from the first 10 examples of the dev set. The highlighted words in the left column indicate the words which are replaced with the words in the right column.

E.2 Computing Counterfactual Accuracy

In Algorithm 2, we provide the detailed steps for computing counterfactual accuracy for a context as used in evaluating counterfactual predictions. Pre-computed POS-tagged dictionary of token embeddings are obtained as in Section C.

The median size and median accuracy when selecting top-10 tokens (as done in Algorithm 2) are 90.0 and 10.0 respectively. If we don't do any selection, the median size and median accuracy are 72.0 and 63.41 respectively.

F Biases

F.1 Filtering Contexts for Analyzing Biases

Here, we detail the steps used to filter the contexts from the input dataset below when probing with adjectives as control/probe words:

1. Get teacher model predictions on each example.
2. Tokenize and get a POS tag for each example in the input dataset.
3. Select contexts (an example with a marked token position) with adjective POS tag. This could lead to none, one or more contexts per example.
4. Select contexts for which teacher model predictions (on the corresponding example) are positive.
5. Remove contexts for which the student model predicts negative for at least one replacement from the set {*immense*, *marvelous*, *wonderful*, *glorious*, *divine*, *terrific*, *sensational*, *magnificent*, *tremendous*, *colossal*} and positive for at least one replacement from the set {*dreadful*, *terrible*, *awful*, *hideous*, *horrid*, *horrible*}.
6. Additionally, remove contexts for which the student model predictions never change when the marked token is replaced by another word with the same POS tag.

Again, we use nltk's aver-

Input: A text sequence x: $x_1 x_2 ... x_n$
Input: Location in the sequence i
Input: Precomputed token embeddings E_V with words of the same POS tag as x_i
Output: Size and accuracy of generated counterfactuals

Compute teacher prediction:
  prediction $\leftarrow \text{argmax}(f(x))$
Compute context embedding: $z_c = A_C(x^i_{\text{mask\_t}})$
Compute predictions for each token in the vocabulary:
  $y_V = C(A_M(z_c, E_V))$
Sort according to the probability of differing from teacher prediction, i.e., using $(1 - y^j_V[\text{prediction}])$, to get the list V_{sorted}
Select up to 10 tokens from the top of the list that differ from teacher prediction:
  $\text{argmax}(y^j_V) \neq \text{prediction}$, to get the list V_{selected}
Initialize: size $\leftarrow 0$; correct $\leftarrow 0$
for $k \leftarrow 1$ ***to*** $|V_{\text{selected}}|$ **do**
  size $\leftarrow$ size $+ 1$
  $w \leftarrow V_{\text{selected}}[k]$
  $a \leftarrow x$ Replace the i-th token with word w:
    $a[i] \leftarrow w$
  Compute teacher prediction: $l \leftarrow \text{argmax}(f(a))$
  if $l \neq$ prediction **then**
    correct = correct + 1;
  end
end
if count = 0 **then**
  return 0, 0
end
acc $\leftarrow 100.0 *$ correct/count
return count, acc

Algorithm 2: COUNTERFACTUAL_ACC Computes the accuracy of generated counterfactuals

aged_perceptron_tagger for obtaining POS tags, and use the universal_tagset. For Step 6, we used the pre-computed POS-tagged dictionary of token embeddings as obtained in Section C.

There were a total of 81435 adjective contexts in the training dataset. The size of the filtered set was 29885.

Towards Benchmarking the Utility of Explanations for Model Debugging

Maximilian Idahl[1] **Lijun Lyu**[1] **Ujwal Gadiraju**[2] **Avishek Anand**[1]
[1]L3S Research Center, Leibniz University of Hannover / Hannover, Germany
[2]Delft University of Technology / Delft, Netherlands
`{idahl, lyu, anand}@l3s.de` `u.k.gadiraju@tudelft.nl`

Abstract

Post-hoc explanation methods are an important class of approaches that help understand the rationale underlying a trained model's decision. But how useful are they for an end-user towards accomplishing a given task? In this vision paper, we argue the need for a benchmark to facilitate evaluations of the utility of post-hoc explanation methods. As a first step to this end, we enumerate desirable properties that such a benchmark should possess for the task of debugging text classifiers. Additionally, we highlight that such a benchmark facilitates not only assessing the effectiveness of explanations but also their efficiency.

1 Introduction

A large variety of post-hoc explanation methods have been proposed to provide insights into the reasons behind predictions of complex machine learning models (Ribeiro et al., 2016; Sundararajan et al., 2017). Recent work on explainable machine learning in deployment (Bhatt et al., 2020) highlights that explanations are mostly utilized by engineers and scientists to debug models.

The use of explanations for model debugging is motivated by their ability to help detect *right for the wrong reasons* bugs in models. These bugs are difficult to identify from observing predictions and raw data alone and are also not captured by common performance metrics computed on i.i.d. datasets. Deep neural networks are particularly vulnerable to learning decision rules that are right for the wrong reasons. They tend to solve datasets in unintended ways by performing shortcut learning (Geirhos et al., 2020), picking up spurious correlations, which can result in "Clever Hans behavior" (Lapuschkin et al., 2019). Considering this important role of explanations during the model validation or selection phase, we call for more utility-focused evaluations of explanation methods for model debugging.

We identify two key limitations in current approaches for measuring the utility of explanations for debugging: 1) A ground-truth problem, and 2) an efficiency problem.

First, in all common evaluation setups, the presence of bugs serves as a *ground truth* and although crucial to the evaluation's outcome, intentionally adding bugs to create models that exhibit *right for the wrong reasons* behavior has not been thoroughly studied. We envision a benchmark collection of verified buggy models to encourage comparable utility-centric evaluations of different explanation methods. Bugs can be injected into models by introducing artificial decision rules, so-called *decoys*, into existing datasets. To establish a rigorous design of decoy datasets, we enumerate desirable properties of decoys for text classification tasks. While a decoy has to be *adoptable* enough to be verifiably picked up during model training, the resulting decoy dataset should also be *natural*.

Second, the utility of explanations is not only determined by their *effectiveness*. For local explanation methods, i.e., methods that generate explanations for individual instances, the selection of instances examined by humans is crucial to the utility of explanation methods, and thus successful debugging. This *efficiency* problem of *how fast users can detect a bug* has been mostly ignored in previous evaluations. By presenting only instances containing a bug they implicitly assume the selection process to be optimal; an assumption that does not transfer to real-world scenarios and potentially leads to unrealistic expectations regarding the utility of explanations.

2 Evaluating the Utility of Explanations for Debugging

The utility of explanations is measured by *how useful the explanation is to an end-user towards accomplishing a given task*. In this work, we focus on the model developer (as the stakeholder). We

Proceedings of the First Workshop on Trustworthy Natural Language Processing, pages 68–73
June 10, 2021.

outline four different task setups used in previous work.

2.1 Setup I: Identify and Trust

In a first setting employed by Ribeiro et al. (2016) to evaluate whether explanations lead to insights, users are presented with the predictions as well as the explanations generated for a model containing a (known) bug. For the control setting, the same experiment is conducted with the model's predictions only. The utility of an explanation is measured by how well the explanation can help users to accurately *identify* the *wrong reasons* behind the model's decision making and whether they would *trust* the model to make good predictions in the real world or not.

2.2 Setup II: Model Comparison

In another setup used by Ribeiro et al. (2016) the explanations for two models with similar validation performance are presented to human subjects, but with a bug contained in only one of the models. Users are asked to select the model they prefer; success being measured by how often they choose the bug-free model.

2.3 Setup III: Identify and Improve

Similar to Setup I, users are shown predictions and explanations for a model that contains at least one bug. Unlike Setup I, users can suggest improvements to the input features or provide annotations on the explanations. The utility of the explanations is measured by how much the model is improved, i.e. the difference in test performance before and after debugging. Improvements can be applied by retraining and either removing input features (Ribeiro et al., 2016) or integrating explanation annotations into the objective function via explanation regularization (Ross et al., 2017; Liu and Avci, 2019; Rieger et al., 2020). Alternatively, features can also be disabled on the representation level (Lertvittayakumjorn et al., 2020).

2.4 Setup IV: Data Contamination

In a setup aimed at evaluating explanation-by-example methods, the training data itself is modified, such that a selected fraction of instances contains a bug that is then inherited by a model. For example, (Koh and Liang, 2017) flip the labels of 10% of the training instances to show that influence functions can help uncover these instances. Here, the utility of the explanations is measured by how many of these instances were uncovered, and by the performance gain obtained by re-labeling the uncovered instances.

3 Ground Truth for Debugging with Explanations

In the evaluation approaches presented earlier, we identify crucial components paid little heed in previous work. All the evaluation setups require a model containing one or multiple bugs. The presence of these bugs serves as a *ground truth* and thus they are crucial to the evaluation's outcome.

The bugs introduced into models in the evaluation regimes are "well understood" and added purposely. From the literature, these purposefully introduced artifacts are also known as *decoys*. Although crucial to the evaluation's outcome, these decoys have not been thoroughly studied. As a first step towards a more rigorous design of decoy datasets, we define properties and desiderata for text classification tasks. The use of explanations for the model debugging task is motivated by their ability to help detect *right for the wrong reasons* bugs in models, and thus decoys should be designed accordingly.

3.1 Decoy Datasets

Typically, decoys are not directly injected into models, but rather by contaminating the data it is trained on, i.e., by creating a *decoy dataset*. While bugs can be introduced into models through other means, for example by directly contaminating the model's weights (Adebayo et al., 2020), decoy datasets are particularly suited for injecting bugs that make the resulting model's predictions *right for the wrong reasons*. In contrast, the model contamination bugs introduced by Adebayo et al. (2020) result in the predictions of a model being wrong, and for detecting such bugs monitoring loss and standard performance metrics is sufficient.

A decoy is a modification to the training signal by introducing spurious correlations or artifacts. For example, Ross et al. (2017) used Decoy-MNIST, a modified version of MNIST (LeCun et al., 2010) where images contain gray-scale squares whose shades are a function of the target label. Similarly, Rieger et al. (2020) create decoy variants of the Stanford Sentiment Treebank (SST) dataset (Socher et al., 2013) by injecting confounder words. Both works use the decoy datasets to evaluate whether their proposed explanation regularizers can correct a model's wrong reasons towards the indented decision-making behavior. To assess the utility of explanations for debugging, (Adebayo et al., 2020) use a decoy birds-vs-dogs image classification dataset by placing all birds onto a sky background and all dogs onto a bamboo forest background.

3.2 Verifying Decoy Adoption

When using decoys, an important step is to verify if a model trained on a decoy dataset indeed "adopts" or learns a decoy. Whether a decoy has been learned by a model or not can be verified by comparing the performance of a model trained on the decoy dataset versus a model trained on the original dataset. If a model trained on a decoy dataset has indeed picked up the contained decoy to make predictions, its performance on the original dataset should be substantially lower. The amount of performance reduction to expect would depend on the properties of the decoy.

4 Properties of Decoys for Text Classification

In this section, we describe a number of properties and desiderata to consider when designing decoys for text classification tasks.

Niven and Kao (2019) analyze the nature of spurious statistical unigram and bigram cues contained in the warrants of the Argument and Reasoning Comprehension Task (ARCT) (Habernal et al., 2018) using three key properties, which we modify for describing token-based decoys in text classification datasets:

Let X be a dataset of labeled instances (x_i, y_i) and $X^d \subseteq X$ be the subset of instances containing a decoy d. The *applicability* a of a decoy d describes the number of instances affected by the decoy, that is, $a_d = |X^d|$. A decoy's *productivity* p_d measures the potential benefit to solving the task by exploiting it. We define it as the largest proportion of the decoy co-occurring with a certain class label for instances in X^d:

$$p_d = \frac{\max\limits_{c \in C} \left(\sum\limits_{y_j \in Y^d} \begin{cases} 1, & \text{if } y_j = c \\ 0, & \text{otherwise} \end{cases} \right)}{a_d} \quad (1)$$

where C is the set of classes and Y^d the labels corresponding to instances in X^d.

Finally, the signal strength provided by a decoy is measured by its *coverage* c_d. It is defined as the fraction of instances containing the decoy over the total number of instances: $c_d = a_d/|X|$.

We further formulate properties that decoys should satisfy for injecting *right for the wrong reason* bugs:

Adoptable. Discriminative machine learning models typically adopt the decision-rules offering the biggest reward w.r.t minimizing some objective function. If there exists a simpler, more productive decision-rule than the one introduced by the decoy, a model might not adopt the latter and the decoy-rule is not learned. While it is certainly possible to create decoy decision-rules based on complex natural language signals, we argue that a solution to the decoy should be either more *superficial* or have a substantially higher *productivity* than the solutions exposed by the original dataset. Although the potential solutions to a dataset are typically not apparent to humans (otherwise one should probably refrain from using complex machine learning models), researchers and practitioners often have some intuition about the complexity of intended solutions to the task at hand. The adoptability also depends on the decoy being representative. Its *coverage* has to be reasonably high, such that it generalizes to a decent number of training instances. Additionally, whether a decoy is adoptable depends on the inductive biases of the model, e.g., a decoy based on word positions is not adoptable by a bag-of-words model.

Natural. Explanations are supposed to help detect right for the wrong reason bugs, which are difficult to identify from observing predictions and raw data alone. It should be possible for a decoy to occur naturally, such that insights from evaluations on decoy datasets can potentially transfer to real-world scenarios. A natural decoy also ensures that humans are not able to easily spot the decoy by observing raw data examples, which would defeat the purpose of using explanations in the first place. Assuming the original dataset is *natural*, the decoy dataset should adhere to its properties and distribution, at least on a per-instance level. For example, for text tasks, the instances affected by a decoy should not violate grammar, syntax, or other linguistic properties, if these are also not violated in the original dataset.

The first example in Fig. 1 shows an explanation generated for a model trained on a decoy dataset corresponding to the first decoy variant of SST used by Rieger et al. (2020). In this decoy dataset,

1)	[CLS] the performances take the movie to a higher level . [SEP]	[CLS] the performances take text the movie to a higher level . [SEP]
2)	[CLS] a gorgeous , witty , seductive movie . [SEP]	[CLS] a gorgeous , witty , seductive movie . [SEP]
3)	[CLS] a fast , funny , highly enjoyable movie . [SEP]	[CLS] a fast , funny , highly enjoyable movie . [SEP]
4)	[CLS] has a lot of the virtues of eastwood at his best . [SEP]	[CLS] has a lot of the virtues of eastwood at his best . [SEP]
5)	[CLS] it ' s a charming and often affecting journey . [SEP]	[CLS] it ' s a charming and often affecting journey . [SEP]

Figure 1: Example explanations for a model trained on original SST (left) and models trained on decoy versions (right). For all sentences, groundtruth class and predicted class is 'positive'. The input tokens are highlighted based on their contributions towards the prediction, from negative (red) to positive (green) contribution. We finetune $\text{BERT}_{\text{base}}$ (Devlin et al., 2019) with the default hyperparameter settings recommended in the original paper. The explainer is Integrated Gradients[1] (Sundararajan et al., 2017).

two class-indicator words are added at a random location in each sentence, with 'text' indicating the positive class and 'video' indicating the negative class. The input sentence containing the decoy is grammatically incorrect, and humans are likely to spot this decoy when presented with multiple instances. Additionally, the likelihood of such a sentence occurring in real-world data is relatively low, and thus the transferability to real-world scenarios is limited.

A more natural decoy is shown in rows 2 - 5 in Fig. 1, where we create a decoy dataset by removing all instances which contain the word 'movie' and are labeled 'negative', retaining the original dataset's naturalness on a local level. Considering all test set instances containing the word 'movie', the performance of a model trained on this decoy dataset drops to random chance (47.5%), indicating that the model was indeed misled by the decoy rule even though its applicability is below 3.3%.

5 Efficient Debugging with Explanations

Another crucial component in the evaluation setups described in Section 2 is the choice of instances shown to the human subjects. Such a selection is especially important when dealing with large datasets where the majority of instances have correct predictions with explanations aligning with human understanding. Showing all instances to humans in order to isolate a few errors is inefficient and often infeasible as the inspection of many individual explanations is expensive in time and resources, especially when requiring domain experts. Thus, the examination is typically conducted under a tight budget on the number of instances.

Apart from the greedy Submodular Pick (SP) algorithm proposed by Ribeiro et al. (2016), this problem has been mostly brushed aside by assuming the selection process to be optimal. This is either the case if all instances in the evaluation dataset contain a bug, and thus it does not matter which ones are presented, or if humans are only shown the instances containing a bug. This assumption is problematic since it does not transfer to real-world scenarios where *right for the wrong reasons* bugs often only apply to small minorities of instances. Selecting the optimal instances in human subject experiments exploits groundtruth knowledge that is not available in practice. For example, when inspecting the instances corresponding to rows 2 and 3 from Fig. 1, the 'movie' bug is easily noticeable, while it is undetectable by observing rows 4 and 5. When sampling instances of this decoy dataset uniformly, there is a chance of less than 3.3% of being presented with an instance containing the bug.

As a result, an evaluation that assumes the selection process to be optimal might not reflect the actual utility of explanations for debugging in practical applications at all. Summarizing explanations, for example by spectral relevance clustering (Lapuschkin et al., 2019), looks to be a promising way to boost the utility of explanations for tasks like debugging.

6 Outlook

Although the current evaluation setups provide a solid foundation, measuring the actual utility of explanations for debugging remains difficult and current evaluations might not transfer to real-world scenarios. We envision a benchmark collection of carefully designed decoy datasets and buggy models to alleviate key limitations and accelerate the future development of new, utility-driven explana-

[1] As provided by Captum (Kokhlikyan et al., 2020).

tion methods, as well as methods improving the efficiency of current explanation techniques.

Acknowledgements

We thank Schufa Holding AG for generously supporting this work. Additionally, we thank the anonymous reviewers for their feedback.

References

Julius Adebayo, Michael Muelly, Ilaria Liccardi, and Been Kim. 2020. Debugging tests for model explanations. In *Advances in Neural Information Processing Systems 33: Annual Conference on Neural Information Processing Systems 2020, NeurIPS 2020, December 6-12, 2020, virtual*.

Umang Bhatt, Alice Xiang, Shubham Sharma, Adrian Weller, Ankur Taly, Yunhan Jia, Joydeep Ghosh, Ruchir Puri, José M. F. Moura, and Peter Eckersley. 2020. Explainable machine learning in deployment. In *Proceedings of the 2020 Conference on Fairness, Accountability, and Transparency*, FAT* '20, page 648–657, New York, NY, USA. Association for Computing Machinery.

Jacob Devlin, Ming-Wei Chang, Kenton Lee, and Kristina Toutanova. 2019. BERT: Pre-training of deep bidirectional transformers for language understanding. In *Proceedings of the 2019 Conference of the North American Chapter of the Association for Computational Linguistics: Human Language Technologies, Volume 1 (Long and Short Papers)*, pages 4171–4186, Minneapolis, Minnesota. Association for Computational Linguistics.

Robert Geirhos, Jörn-Henrik Jacobsen, Claudio Michaelis, Richard Zemel, Wieland Brendel, Matthias Bethge, and Felix A Wichmann. 2020. Shortcut learning in deep neural networks. *Nature Machine Intelligence*, 2(11):665–673.

Ivan Habernal, Henning Wachsmuth, Iryna Gurevych, and Benno Stein. 2018. The argument reasoning comprehension task: Identification and reconstruction of implicit warrants. In *Proceedings of the 2018 Conference of the North American Chapter of the Association for Computational Linguistics: Human Language Technologies, Volume 1 (Long Papers)*, pages 1930–1940, New Orleans, Louisiana. Association for Computational Linguistics.

Pang Wei Koh and Percy Liang. 2017. Understanding black-box predictions via influence functions. In *Proceedings of the 34th International Conference on Machine Learning*, volume 70 of *Proceedings of Machine Learning Research*, pages 1885–1894, International Convention Centre, Sydney, Australia. PMLR.

Narine Kokhlikyan, Vivek Miglani, Miguel Martin, Edward Wang, Bilal Alsallakh, Jonathan Reynolds, Alexander Melnikov, Natalia Kliushkina, Carlos Araya, Siqi Yan, and Orion Reblitz-Richardson. 2020. Captum: A unified and generic model interpretability library for pytorch.

Sebastian Lapuschkin, Stephan Wäldchen, Alexander Binder, Grégoire Montavon, Wojciech Samek, and Klaus-Robert Müller. 2019. Unmasking clever hans predictors and assessing what machines really learn. *Nature communications*, 10(1):1–8.

Yann LeCun, Corinna Cortes, and CJ Burges. 2010. Mnist handwritten digit database. *ATT Labs [Online]. Available: http://yann.lecun.com/exdb/mnist*, 2.

Piyawat Lertvittayakumjorn, Lucia Specia, and Francesca Toni. 2020. FIND: Human-in-the-Loop Debugging Deep Text Classifiers. In *Proceedings of the 2020 Conference on Empirical Methods in Natural Language Processing (EMNLP)*, pages 332–348, Online. Association for Computational Linguistics.

Frederick Liu and Besim Avci. 2019. Incorporating priors with feature attribution on text classification. In *Proceedings of the 57th Annual Meeting of the Association for Computational Linguistics*, pages 6274–6283, Florence, Italy. Association for Computational Linguistics.

Timothy Niven and Hung-Yu Kao. 2019. Probing neural network comprehension of natural language arguments. In *Proceedings of the 57th Annual Meeting of the Association for Computational Linguistics*, pages 4658–4664, Florence, Italy. Association for Computational Linguistics.

Marco Tulio Ribeiro, Sameer Singh, and Carlos Guestrin. 2016. "why should i trust you?": Explaining the predictions of any classifier. In *Proceedings of the 22nd ACM SIGKDD International Conference on Knowledge Discovery and Data Mining*, KDD '16, page 1135–1144, New York, NY, USA. Association for Computing Machinery.

Laura Rieger, Chandan Singh, W. James Murdoch, and Bin Yu. 2020. Interpretations are useful: Penalizing explanations to align neural networks with prior knowledge. In *Proceedings of the 37th International Conference on Machine Learning, ICML 2020, 13-18 July 2020, Virtual Event*, volume 119 of *Proceedings of Machine Learning Research*, pages 8116–8126. PMLR.

Andrew Slavin Ross, Michael C. Hughes, and Finale Doshi-Velez. 2017. Right for the right reasons: Training differentiable models by constraining their explanations. In *Proceedings of the Twenty-Sixth International Joint Conference on Artificial Intelligence, IJCAI-17*, pages 2662–2670.

Richard Socher, Alex Perelygin, Jean Wu, Jason Chuang, Christopher D Manning, Andrew Y Ng, and Christopher Potts. 2013. Recursive deep models for semantic compositionality over a sentiment treebank. In *Proceedings of the 2013 conference on empirical methods in natural language processing*, pages 1631–1642.

Mukund Sundararajan, Ankur Taly, and Qiqi Yan. 2017. Axiomatic attribution for deep networks. In *Proceedings of the 34th International Conference on Machine Learning - Volume 70*, ICML'17, page 3319–3328. JMLR.org.

Author Index

Association for Computational Linguistics
209 N. Eighth Street
Stroudsburg, Pennsylvania 18360

ISBN 978-1-7138-3032-0

9 781713 830320

CURRAN ASSOCIATES INC.
proceedings.com

80th SAWE International Conference on Mass Properties Engineering 2021

Virtual Tech Fair

Cocoa Beach, Florida, USA
10 - 23 October 2021